Harold W. Demone, Jr., Ph.D.
Dwight Harshbarger, Ph.D.

THE PLANNING
AND ADMINISTRATION
OF HUMAN SERVICES

A SEPARATE OF VOLUME I IN

developments in
HUMAN SERVICES

Edited by
Herbert C. Schulberg, Ph.D.
Frank Baker, Ph.D.
Sheldon R. Roen, Ph.D.

THE PLANNING AND ADMINISTRATION OF HUMAN SERVICES

by
**Harold W. Demone, Jr., Ph.D.
and Dwight Harshbarger, Ph.D.**

(Part II of Developments in Human Services,
Volume 1,
Edited by
Herbert C. Schulberg, Ph.D.,
Frank Baker, Ph.D., and
Sheldon R. Roen, Ph.D.

Library of Congress Catalog Card Number 73-6870
Standard Book Number 87705-077-5
Copyright © 1973 by Behavioral Publications

BEHAVIORAL PUBLICATIONS, 2852 Broadway—Morningside Heights,
New York, New York 10025

Printed in the United States of America

Library of Congress Cataloging in Publication Data

Demone, Harold W
    The planning and administration of human services.

    Also issued in v. 1 of Developments in human services
    1. Social service.   2. Social work administration.
I. Harshbarger, Dwight, joint author.   II. Title.
[HV40.D45]   361   73-6870

CONTENTS

PREFACE TO THE SEPARATES OF THE "DEVELOPMENTS IN HUMAN SERVICES" SERIES

Widespread inadequacies in the human condition, and concern for the difficulties and complexities of existing social arrangements, have created urgent pressures upon professionals to revise present care-giving mechanisms. Human service programs such as multi-service centers, which incorporate a wide variety of relevant services, are emerging as an alternative framework to the existing pattern of rigid, categorical services for meeting the bio-psycho-social needs of individuals and populations.

The editors of this new encyclopedic series have undertaken to develop materials which can serve as guide posts for those newly entering or already engaged in the field of human services. A flexible approach to the production and distribution of these materials has been devised.

The plan for the series is to publish annually indepth discussions and reviews on the following human service topics:

—Emerging Conceptions of human service such as systems and ecological frameworks
—Administrative and planning tools such as information systems, economic strategies, and legal mechanisms
—Innovative service programs within new organizational models and new communities
—Educational programs for changing professional roles and new manpower requirements

After several years, those who are standing order subscribers will possess an encyclopedic library of human services in either hardbound volumes or softcover separates.

The first volume contains an introductory overview by the editors, four substantitive sections on different human service topics as enumerated below, and a comprehensive index. Each of the substantitive sections, without introductory overview and index, are available as separates. These are:

Teaching Health and Human Services Administration by the Case Method
    Linda G. Sprague, Alan Sheldon, M.D., and Curtis P. McLaughlin, D.B.A.

The Planning and Administration of Human Services
    Harold W. Demone, Jr., Ph.D. and Dwight Harshbarger, Ph.D.

Strategies in Innovative Human Service Programs
    Harry Gottesfeld, Ph.D., Florence Lieberman, D.S.W., Sheldon R. Roen, Ph.D., and Sol Gordon, Ph.D.

Developments in Human Services Education and Manpower
    Robert M. Vidaver, M.D.

                                                    The Editors

1. HUMAN NEEDS AND HUMAN SERVICES ORGANIZATIONS

The next decade will severely test the fabric of American society. A number of important current questions will be answered differently during this period, and the outcomes will hold major significance for the direction and stability of America. We should become more certain of the conditions under which it might be possible for cities to support meaningful, productive life styles, or whether they will become burnt-out shells—depressing monuments to societal indecision, error, and poor planning. We should be better able to determine the extent to which public schools might become sources of excitement and meaningful learning or whether those that remain will provide prototypic social paradigms for uncritical conformity and limited intellectual vision. We will become more and more painfully aware of the serious limitations of our inadequate and overburdened health delivery systems. Whether or not new models of health delivery systems will emerge, survive, and actually deliver health services without discriminating on the basis of ethnicity and income should become evident during these years.

These represent only a few of the extremely serious questions confronting American society. Racism and more subtle but equally devastating forms of ethnic prejudice continue to plague our social and economic relationships. Generations of Americans in inner cities and regions such as Appalachia are being socialized into life styles that have at their core a dependency on outdated, dysfunctional, and demeaning systems of welfare. And vast numbers of middle-class citizens, on entering mental health settings, are asking why affluence does not produce feelings of "the good life."

The abuses of alcohol and, more recently, drugs continue annually to inhibit large numbers of persons from engaging in meaningful lives. Correctional institutions appear to be little more than a significant bench mark in the life of a criminal, a kind of alma mater to which he returns periodically for continuing education. Mental hospitals, despite often dramatic changes during the 1960s, continue to place a very disabling stigma on former patients. Whether or not community mental health centers will, nationally, become more than a subsidy for middle-class therapists' office space or alternatively small state hospitals is still an open question. And after almost a decade of community mental health most state mental health departments still spend 90% of their budgets on institutions and despite decreasing censuses continue to act as if the state hospital remains their principal form of intervention.

The common thread running through all of these problems is that they are being dealt with by what might be described as human services organizations, that is, by organizations in the public or voluntary sector that have as their mandate primary, secondary, and tertiary prevention of biosocial problems. Moreover, they carry the implicit mandate that their combined efforts should contribute to the improvement of the general social welfare and the development of proadaptive or active, rather than passive, ecological behaviors among a population.

Within the broad framework of comprehensive health and welfare services these organizations have been given substantial responsibilities for *(a)* the prevention or lowering of incidences of certain problems, *(b)* the reduction of the duration of occurring problems, and *(c)* the rehabilitation of persons who have experienced selected problems in living.

Using a comprehensive definition of human services, one that might include such apparently diverse socializing organizations as prisons, mental hospitals, rehabilitative services, and public schools, these organizations are expected to produce behavior repertoires among people that lead to their dealing with their personal environments in such a way that they can gain some control over their own destinies and exercise some freedom of choice in their lives.

All industrialized societies have found it necessary to create some system of health, educational, and welfare services. Some have become more complex and elaborate than others (e.g., the United States is the only industrialized country in the world that does not have a system of national health insurance), and there are differences in both the efficiency and effectiveness in the operations of these organizations. However, they are omnipresent in all industrialized countries.

These organizations, with few exceptions, have been funded and operated by varying combinations of federal, state, local, and voluntary funds. Their origins and growth patterns have generally coincided with the development and/or recognition of human problems in industrial society. Welfare systems arose around the themes of children, the aged, and poverty and were principally oriented toward providing some means of support for poor and orphaned children. It should be noted that an orphaned child probably would not have found himself without human resources in an earlier, preindustrialized society. Rather, some subunit of his family, in the extended family structure of that period, would have taken him into their home. Formal societal intervention would not have been necessary. However, industrialization created mobility patterns that severely hampered the classic extended family. Thus, if social intervention was to occur, it became increasingly necessary for this function to be taken on by formally organized nonfamilial complex organizations. (In a sense it is a bit surprising that the rudiments of a human service system emerged at all, given the Protestant ethic of individualized competition and achievement and the ideology of social Darwinism that prevailed at the turn of the century. Perhaps the key variable, after all, was the spirit of humanitarianism.)

The pattern is to identify a biosocial problem, followed by public and professional concern and concluding with the development of a categorical delivery system. As industrialization and the complexity of work, residential, and mobility patterns increased, larger amounts of national resources have been allocated to organized attempts at problem remediation. Over the last few years the average annual growth of the health industry has been 11%.

In order for a human services organization to arise, it is, and has been, necessary for legislative or other bodies formally representing communities to appropriate monies for support. (Free-standing, categorical fund-raising efforts soliciting funds directly from the public have seldom had a major impact on problems, even though substantial amounts of money have been raised collectively.) In turn, funds have been most likely appropriated in those problem areas that could be empirically verified and that held the potential for solidifying a base of political support—most evident during the depression and the years of the Roosevelt administration, a time of both unprecedented expansion of human services in the welfare sector and a vast expansion in the numbers of people who identified with and voted for, the Democratic party.

Such a remedial, reactive orientation toward social problems and the need to maintain a consumer constituency have been major factors in the development of human service systems. The debates about welfare and national health insurance also illustrate these principles. Such factors have played powerful roles in continuing the tendency to react to problems by developing organizations to remediate rather than generating thrusts in the direction of altering molar patterns of human ecology that might reduce the prevalence of such problems.

The history of human services organizations in America has not been particularly distinguished. Attempts to deal with complex and vexing social problems have been generally reactive and consistently underfinanced, understaffed, and lacking access to avenues of power in the private sector that might bring about significant partnerships for change in social systems. But however myopic our vision might have been, it has not been lost. Substantial amounts of resources are currently being channeled into human service organizations. Approximately one-third of our over $700 billion gross national product (GNP) is being spent in the human services. (Whatever the values of such statistics, some absurdities are built into the data. For example, we include in the GNP both the wages paid to a coal miner and expenditures by former miners to delay and make as painless as possible their deaths from "black lung.") Massive and sometimes powerful human service organizations do exist. The potential for biosocial intervention and change is present. It may be that an adequate proportion of the GNP is presently invested, but this will never be known with our present dysfunctional delivery system.

THE HUMAN SERVICES
ORGANIZATION: WHAT IS IT?

In beginning the study of human service organizations, it is important to realize that they are both similar and different from other complex organizations. They share problems of differentiation-integration (e.g., Lawrence & Lorsch, 1967), resource acquisition (e.g., Rice, 1958), and role strain and role conflict (Biddle & Thomas, 1966). They also differ along important dimensions, which in turn give human service organizations a highly unique character. There are complex organizations, and there are complex organizations.

One of the most important characteristics of an organization is the development and use of criteria that provide information feedback to that organization and serve as indicators that shape organizational policy decisions. They have assumed two primary forms: *(a)* economic indices, usually assuming the form of profits or some relative comparisons of organizational income to payments; and *(b)* programmatic outcome indices that show the impact of an organization on its target environment, such as changes in the number of products sold to or consumed by a given population, changes in recidivism rates, changes in academic achievement test scores, etc.

Although these criteria are relatively easily developed in, say, business organizations, they are quite problematic for most human service organizations. Some proprietary (profit-making) institutions do exist in the human service industry. Proprietary hospitals are a classic example, although nursing homes may be the largest single class. Most recently day-care and homemaker services have been offered by major profit-making organizations. Generally, however, human services organizations are supported out of public and voluntary resources and do not expect to make a profit. Neither can they tally indicators of their effectiveness as easily as a sales manager charts the sales of new cars. What kinds of feedback might indicate to a welfare agency that it is having a desired impact on a community? Case load? Changes in case loads? Migratory patterns among welfare recipients? Similarly, how might a community mental health center examine its roles and impact in community life? By the number of persons requiring hospitalization? Patients remaining in treatment? Changes in rates of alcoholism and drug addiction? Crime rates? Church attendance? Divorce rates? What are the indicators of meaningful, productive community lives?

Whatever the political dimensions underlying human service organizations, their origins seem to lie in social values. Health, education, and welfare organizations generally express societal concern. And although the concerns and values operate to provide a general base of public support, operationalizing these values in such a way that the impact of an organization can be reliably and validly assessed is a major problem for virtually all human service organizations. To a large extent these problems have been largely ignored by human service organizations. (Who has seriously questioned our system of public education?) We have not, until recently, begun to conscientiously deal with the problems of program outcomes, community social indicators, and a level of analysis of organizational impact that goes beyond simple health indicators, welfare case loads, and educational test scores. Instead, we have developed elaborate and often ritualized professional organizations, identities, and behaviors (see, e.g., Goffman, 1961; Harshbarger, 1970a) among the actors in human services organizations. These, in turn, have often taken on a life of their own and have become the criteria by which an organization is judged by those who must make resource allocation decisions.

These underlying factors create some important and unique taxonomic dimensions in human services organizations. The following comparisons between private (profit) sector, production-oriented organizations, and public-private (nonprofit) sector, human services organizations indicate some of these organizational differences (Harshbarger, 1970b).

Collectively, these dimensions lead to nonprofit, public, and voluntary organizations that have a nature and character that generally differentiate them from profit-making organizations. Their actors perform their roles within professional-organizational sanctions and safeguards that protect them from the viscissitudes and vagaries of political pressures that might be brought to bear on actors in other types of organizations. Physicians, teachers, social workers, nurses, psychologists, and many other professionalized employee groups account to each other via their professional organizations and to their organization's funding sources in terms of criteria that have typically been professionally developed, sanctioned, and legitimized. They control the crea-

TABLE 1

Private, profit sector, production organizations	Public-voluntary, non-profit sector, human services organizations
The organization is structured and organized in accordance with production cycles-systems.	The organization is structured and organized in accordance with professional values and membership subgroupings.
Organizationally defined tasks provide the primary bases of social segregation and interaction.	Professional membership groups provide the primary basis of social segregation and interaction. Task definition is usually developed by these groups.
Social hierarchies and social power are based in the formal organizational distribution of power.	Social hierarchies and social power are based in professional hierarchies and their relative possession of power.
Intraorganizational norms and behaviors are largely based in production standards of desired efficiency (in both formal and informal organizational subsystems).	Intraorganizational norms and behaviors are largely based in the values of professional and organizational membership groups.
The first allegiance of an individual is to his organizational membership group.	The first allegiance of an individual is to his professional membership group.
The allegiance of the individual to the organization is assumed and is not an area of major conflict.	The allegiance of the individual to the organization is problematical and may be an area of major conflict.
No (or very limited) use of job tenure.	Widespread use of job tenure.
Organizational and role performance of the individual is assessed by a profit criterion.	Organizational performance of the individual is assessed by criteria based in professional value judgments.
The consumption of materials is end-product oriented.	The consumption of materials is means or process oriented.
Relatively clear definition of the end product(s).	Relatively unclear definition of the end product(s).
Cost-effectiveness indices are relatively easily developed.	Cost-effectiveness indices are difficult or impossible to develop; the major problem is the measure of effectiveness.
The overall mission or purpose of the organization is established by a small group (e.g., board of	The overall mission or purpose of the organization is established by a relatively large group (e.g.,

directors) that acts in the best interests of the organization and its ownership. The primary criterion for the development of new purposes for the organization is that of organizational survival.	legislators) that acts in the best interests of the public and that often has conflicting interests. The primary criterion for the development of new purposes for the organization is public interest. It is assumed that meeting public needs will give certainty to organizational survival.

tion of, and access to, data that are indicative of organizational performance. In short, these organizations and their resident professionals have, through the design and control of information-feedback systems, far greater control over the social construction of organizational reality than is exercised by actors in other kinds of organizations. The major exception is the research-consultation-oriented profit-making organization whose professional employees manifest the same role strains and whose management must accommodate to the process of dual identification.

ISSUES AND PROBLEMS

The Dilemma of Stability and Change

With a few notable exceptions, effective civil service regulations and organized professional groups have acted as stabilizing influences in most federal, state, and local human services organizations. Political patronage has been reduced to a point that, in most states, a change in state or local government elected officialdom does not appreciably affect the community programs of a human service organization. Simultaneously, there has been an increase in the degree to which these organizations have become staffed by persons labeled as professionals.

Although these factors have created intraorganizational stability and integrity, the environment surrounding human services organizations has undergone major and radical changes in recent years. Emery and Trist (1965)

have described these changes in environmental texture
as increases in environmental turbulence.

At a broad community level, we face the very difficult
problem of meaningfully joining communities that seem
to have lost their sense of direction in the midst of a
storm and community human service organizations that
are capable of navigating only in relatively untroubled
waters.

One major issue of the present and the foreseeable future is whether or not human services organizations can
move out of their often traditional molds and develop
strategies for a very rapidly changing society. The difficulties involved in this process are multiple. Representative problems include the development of change mechanisms that will be effective in what are often highly in-
sular organizations such as schools and hospitals; that
do not alienate organizational constituencies; that do not
eliminate the best of organizational programs in order to
eliminate the worst; and that promise reasonable stability during the change process and do not make life so un-
comfortable for organizational actors that, through a
combination of attrition and anxiety, the organization is
rendered ineffective. Those same mechanisms that have
reduced political influence in human services organizations have contributed to a system that has become more
responsive to its own needs than to those of the consumer. For example, the public human service administrator is faced with multiple constituencies; first are the
employees, next are federal peers, then are his elected
officials, fourth are the clients, and last are the taxpayers. Inevitable conflict of interest is the result.

The Problems of Resource Acquisition and Alloca-
tion

The first job of every administrator is to continually
monitor the external environment of the organization to
maintain the flow of resources into the organization.
Any decrease in either the level or reliability of resources

will have real consequences in terms of positions and programs in his organization.

During the past decade the level of funding for the human services has expanded considerably. U.S. health expenditures alone increased from approximately $23 billion in 1960 to over $60 billion in 1970. Yet in 1970 in the United States a 10-year-old boy had a shorter life expectancy than in 21 other countries in the world; 12 countries had lower rates of infant mortality; one-sixth of all admissions to Cook County Hospital in Chicago died; and there was a purported national shortage of 50,000 physicians and 200,000 nurses as the system was organized. The entire structure of our health-care system is open to question.

The stagnation of the inner city and the decline of rural populations have jointly brought into question major issues in mobility, residential patterns, and adequate schools while financially exhausting our welfare systems.

Although resources have increased, the frequency, intensity, and complexity of the problems that face us have increased at a much more rapid rate. Even a three- or fourfold increase in human service funding patterns over 10 years may be inadequate in view of the exponential increases in the biosocial community problems facing human service organizations.

It may be that increases in funding simply cannot keep pace with increases in problems. If that is the case, administrators of problem-focused human services organizations will have to seriously re-examine that organization's operating and survival strategies. What will be the organizational and community consequences of maintaining present patterns of community resource allocations? What are the implications in continuing existing organizations and their respective approaches to community problems? Is it likely that multiple agencies will continue to compete for funds under conditions of relative scarcity, or might they work out, through new program designs, mutually compatible patterns of sharing resources? Might they work out such patterns if the consequences involve the demise of one of those organizations? Is it possible to generate new models of human services organizations under these conditions?

Which Organizations Shall Survive?

It would seem obvious at this point in time that we are desperately in need of a substantial reorganization in the human services. In many areas this is beginning to occur and hopefully will maximize the effective use of human services resources. However, the problem is how decisions are to be made regarding what specifically is to be reorganized and how that is to be accomplished. What are our criteria? How can we assess the impact of human services organizations in communities?

Gathering the appropriate data to make decisions regarding these problems has been problematic. The secrecy of many agencies regarding data on their activities in communities is understandable, given the potential consequences of openness; that is, they might find this data used as evidence for some other agency's effectiveness and their own relative ineffectiveness. It is probable that funding authorities (e.g., legislatures, United Funds) will have to force a level of organizational disclosure that is unprecedented.

Simultaneously, there will need to be developed more effective indicators and criteria that can put available data to use in assessing both community needs and problems, as well as organizational impact on those problems. Presently, we do not have sufficiently valid biosocial indicators to suggest much more than problem severity. We are unable to look at new models of organizations and programs and make reasonable probability statements about the impact and effectiveness of proposed models.

Such indicators are a must. They are a vital but missing element in the maturation of potentially valuable systems-analytic models or organizations and communities. The beginnings have been made. (See, e.g., Baker & Schulberg, pp. 182-206, 1970; Baker, 1970.) Much more is needed, and it is needed rapidly. For cautions see Noble, (1971).

Planning

In designing the structure and functions of human service organizations, the last unit that is usually added is one relating to planning. (Operational research has a slightly higher priority.) When and if operating funds are reduced in the future, it is likely that this will be the first unit to feel the impact of these restrictions. To the business-oriented executive, planning is equated with product development, an overhead item to be vigorously controlled. As is the case with many minority groups, planners are the last to be hired and the first to be fired.

Yet planning is a vital element in program development. It is even more critical during periods of budgetary limitations and major social change, such as the present, when the soundest thinking should be going into the development of medium-range goals and programs. It is somewhat paradoxical that budgetary restrictions are likely to lower the priorities on planning and the number of staff members involved in planning at the very time when planning effective strategies of survival is most critical to the organization.

In rearranging organizational priorities having to do with planning, it would seem adaptively functional to combine in one unit those positions having to do with both operational research and planning. In effect, this would place in one administrative structure the organizational functions of information feedback and the organizational guidance system. Although one often finds this to be the case, research and planning offices are as likely to be found in separate, often relatively noncommunicating parts of an organization. This makes about as much sense as designing in a rocket environmental monitoring information feedback systems that operate independently from the guidance system. Yet it is precisely this kind of functional independence that characterizes relationships between program researchers and planners in many human services organizations.

In an era in which environmental turbulence is making it extremely difficult, if not impossible, to develop long-range plans, it would seem important that short- and middle-range plans be the best that they can be. Perhaps it is only a question of whether organizational growth will assume the form of maximal or minimal "disjointed incrementalism" (Braybrooke & Lindbloom, 1963). If that is the case, then it becomes even more essential that resources, which seem to be rapidly diminishing relative to the immensity of problem increases, be used in the most rational manner possible.

2. ORGANIZATIONAL ISSUES

As indicated earlier, the human services organization exists and operates within parameters that give this organization a unique character. The human service organization is seldom required to make a profit. Nor are the results of its efforts customarily clearcut and tangible. Often it must survive in an environment of social-political pressures; of conflicting constituencies; of sit-ins; of high-level executive appointments and summary dismissals; of middle-level civil service rules and tenure; and of professional standards. Not surprisingly, the organizational problems that it must face, although in some ways similar to other forms of organizations, have a uniqueness that reflects the nature and character of this form of organization.

ORGANIZATIONAL MODELS— ISSUES AND ALTERNATIVES

As with other forms of social organization, the human service agency must be structured to fulfill certain functions. It must be able to deal with change, anticipated and unanticipated, in the external interorganizational environment. If the organization is designed to be responsive, changes in the surrounding political system should not disrupt it severely. Less flexible structures may suffer severe organizational strains.

At the same time, internal organizational stability must be developed and maintained. There must be a relatively reliable and internally consistent division of labor and differentiation of roles. Predictability and flexibility are required simultaneously.

These two factors, internal and external organizational reliability, are paramount in the development of an effective model of a human services organization. If there is no reliability, then an organization cannot be expected to fulfill even the simplest of missions. Neither people nor organizations will perform rationally and consistently under conditions of environmental uncertainty or unreliability.

Yet decisions regarding the real or potential predictability of these functions cannot be limited exclusively to intraorganizational issues. No organization exists in isolation. An organizational chart, complete with accurate diagrams of functional pathways of communication and decision-making, cannot by itself yield valid information on which predictions about an organization's performance can be based. The first, and most important, consideration is one concerned with the environment in which the organization must survive. Given the external demands generated by survival itself, how should an organization be structured? What kind of internal structure is necessary to withstand the buffeting of the outer environment? What kind of internal structure will best glean available resources from the outer environment?

Decisions that create new organizational structures, whether as reorganizations of or additions to existing organizations, or as new organizations, are filled with risk. And although these decisions are of tremendous import, they tend to be made in relative haste. Too often, environmental pressures and internal structural strains have been neglected, only to return to haunt the organization's inhabitants.

Every organization will, within rather wide limits, take whatever steps are necessary to maintain itself. It will, if necessary, expend inordinate resources to continue its existence. And the larger the proportion of resources that are required for organizational maintenance, the smaller the proportion of resources that are available for goal attainment. The consequences of decisions about organizational structure and real and lasting in their effects.

There is abundant information that would suggest that many past models of human services organizations have not been particularly effective in meeting their organizational and sociocultural goals; for example, the poor are receiving medical care that does not begin to approach minimal acceptable levels; the cost escalation is making medical services a luxury even for the middle class; although mental institutions consume over 90% of most state mental health budgets, few provide services other than institutionalization; educational systems are outdated and antiquated; and welfare reform has become a major national effort.

In each of these cases we are, in the 1970s, dealing with organizational models in which the basic form was usually designed prior to the turn of the century. (Welfare, the most contemporary model, was last fashioned in the 1930s.) They have become organizational dinosaurs, consuming quantities of resources that are vastly disproportional to their social utility.

Only one state, California, in 1970, has passed legislation that may, through the use of medical paraprofessionals, broaden the base of its medical care. Only one state, North Dakota, in 1968, has begun a serious effort to reorganize its educational system. National health insurance and welfare reform still await action by Congress.

At local and regional levels decision-making processes regarding new and modified organizational structures have lacked maps and compasses that might serve as effective guides to the decision-making process. Too often there has been no framework within which there might be a concerting of decisions in the public interest. Rather, well-intentioned decisions have been made in quarters far removed from third parties, such as consumers and other human services organizations, who will be directly affected by these decisions.

It would seem appropriate that decisions regarding human service organizational structures, particularly in the development of new organizations, should be made within some kind of general systems framework, one that attempts to define, integrate, and interdigitate available resources, target populations, present delivery systems and capabilities, felt consumer needs, and organizational needs. It makes little sense for communities to attempt to add additional physicians to an already overburdened and inadequate model of service delivery; it makes little sense to expand a welfare system that has outcomes that rarely go beyond maintaining sustenance among its clients; it also makes little sense to add another school to an educational system that is based on a nineteenth-century philosophy of education.

Specifically, the following considerations should be included in decisions regarding the structuring of new, or the restructuring of old, human services organizations:

1. Can the target population be defined? Are there patterns, such as age or career, that help define any movement in or out of this target population and might serve as points of maximally effective intervention?

2. What is the target system? What are the sources of its funds? Where are decisions of resource allocation made? What are subdivisions of the system? How are the units related? What kinds of exchanges are transacted?

3. What are the system goals? What are specific goals of subunits within the target system? Can these goals be organized in a manner that is consistent with the needs of the target population? How much redundancy is there? What elements within the target population are actually affected by these goals?

4. What are the external system relationships? What functions outside of services themselves must be maintained in order to ensure the survival of the target system?

5. What are some outcomes of services that might be agreed on by all parties involved with the new or restructured organization?

In short, what is the context in which a new or modified organization must survive? What are the systemic community and interorganizational properties of that environment?

If most of these questions cannot be answered satisfactorily, then it makes as little sense to develop a new neighborhood storefront or multi-service center as it does to add one more unit to a highly bureaucratized and centralized organization.

INTERORGANIZATIONAL PROBLEMS

Slowly, over the past 10 years, there has begun to emerge a language that may ultimately permit the articulation of interorganizational relationships. This language, partially based on general systems and social systems theories is aimed at developing multilevel conceptions of interorganizational relationships, dependencies, and resource exchanges. Conceptual papers by Levine and White (1961), Litwak and Hylton (1962), Evan (1966), Gross (1967), Warren (1967), and Baker and Schulberg (1970, pp. 182-206) are representative of these developments.

At a community and interorganizational level the problems faced by human service organizations are different, depending on the kinds of interorganizational relationships that have been worked out in the past. Following Warren's (1967) treatment of the ways in which interorganizational units interact in the decision-making process, we might find four types of decision-making contexts: *(a)* a unitary context, for example, a city health authority in which the units are organized for the achievement of inclusive goals; *(b)* a federative context, for example, a council of social agencies in which each unity has its own goals but that share some formal organization for the accomplishment of inclusive goals; *(c)* a coalitional context, for example, a health planning committee in which participating units cooperate to attain some desired objective, but informally and on an *ad hoc* basis; and *(d)* a social-choice context in which organizations may relate around a certain issue, although they do not necessarily share any inclusive goals and in which authority rests at the unit level.

Each of these contexts defines a kind of interorganizational environment, a set of relationships that carries certain assets and liabilities and places certain kinds of parameters on the participating organizations.

These interorganizational relationships are likely to take place in differing kinds of community environments. Emery and Trist (1965) described four types of environmental causal textures or areas of interdependencies that are characteristic of the environment itself: *(a)* a placid, randomized environment in which there are few disturbances and resources are distributed randomly; *(b)* a placid, clustered environment in which there are few disturbances but in which resources are distributed nonrandomly; *(c)* a disturbed-reactive environment in which similar units, or organizations, compete for available resources; *(d)* a turbulent field in which there is both a competition for resources and, simultaneously, a number of changes in the environmental field itself.

Terreberry (1968) has suggested that organizations are experiencing increasingly turbulent environments. Human services organizations in urban areas are finding themselves having to compete for limited resources and at the same time deal with the dynamic properties of a rapidly changing social environment.

Human services organizations, within these multilevel community and interorganizational contexts, find themselves entering into relationships and decisions that are aimed at multilevel outcomes. Such outcomes might be approached in terms of their relevance to community needs, interorganizational relationships, and intraorganizational needs. In approaching these problems and in entering into decisions about meeting community needs, each human services organization hopes to enhance its resources through interorganizational decisions and resource exchanges.

These transactions, or exchanges, Levine and White (1961) have noted, assume three primary forms: *(a)* clients, *(b)* labor services, and *(c)* resources other than labor services. Although the first two can be documented and empirically demonstrated relatively easily, it is the latter category that is probably the most intangible, yet the most important, in the life of an organization. The components of exchange in this category will differ, depending on the nature of the human services organization, but will include vitally important exchanges such as those relating to political support, as well as other exchanges having to do with exchanges of information about clients, other organizations, etc.

In a community an organization ordinarily directs its principal efforts at survival and growth. For human services organizations one method will be to attempt to increase resources by directly meeting community needs (e.g., fees for service, increased United Fund support); in part, these efforts will be aimed at negotiating productive, profitable trade-offs of organizational resources. A partly qualifying trend just beginning to surface is the refusal of some organizations to grow on "soft" money (having already suffered cash flow problems or funds dried up in policy shifts) or on funds that require major intraorganizational changes or long-range commitments.

INTRAORGANIZATIONAL PROBLEMS

As the external requirements, or parameters, that operate on and around an organization assume some structure or form, internal organizational positions, roles, and norms begin to emerge. Over time the tasks people perform and the ways in which they relate to each other become sufficiently routinized to allow for necessary levels of predictability in everyday organizational life. Imbedded in these developmental processes are both the elements that are required for long-term organizational stability, goal-setting, and growth, as well as the potential for excessive routinization, bureaucratic red tape, boredom, and organizational dry rot (Gardner, 1965). It is this dilemma that confronts all organizations, large and small.

Every organization is at some time engaged in the difficult process of making decisions about its centralization or decentralization, formal or informal organizational demands, performances of old tasks or searches for new ones, maintaining organizational sanctions or changing these sanctions, and maintaining patterns of authority and decision-making or changing those patterns. These are but a few of the issues that center around maintaining internal organizational reliability in an interorganizational environment that is changing and placing new demands on its component organizations.

Terreberry (1968) has suggested that most major internal organizational change is induced through changes in the organization's external environment. Recent experiences in the field of mental health would support her position. Through the development of effective and decentralized community mental health programs in such places as the Canadian Province of Saskatchewan and the states of California and Minnesota and the advent of new chemotherapies, mental hospitals have found themselves with dwindling rates of patient input and increasing rates of patient output. In Saskatchewan the result has been the closing of some hospitals and a radical reorganization of others to accommodate a different patient population. Minnesota and California have experienced a similar phenomenon.

Most human services organizations, however, are neither quite as antiquated nor as likely to be as drastically affected by environmental changes as the traditional mental hospital structure. Most human services organizations, for example, rehabilitation services and welfare systems, are sufficiently in touch with their interorganizational, socio-politico-economic environments to be somewhat responsive to changing demands but sufficiently bounded by protective mechanisms and constituencies to prevent the generation of major internal organizational changes.

Within most human services organizations two kinds of internal regulatory devices operate to place limits and sanctions on intraorganizational behavior: *(a)* a bureaucratized organizational structure and *(b)* professionalization of staff members. In examining the problem of social regulation in organizations, Hall (1967) has indicated that in an organization's effort to maintain some level of intraorganizational reliability and /or social control, an organization will rely on professional norms and standards if possible; if this is not possible, then hierarchical, bureaucratized systems will emerge. The greater the degree of professionalization the lesser the bureaucratic hierarchy; conversely, the lesser the degree of professionalization, the greater the degree of bureaucratization.

By definition, an organization is a regulated system of behaviors and exchanges. In a human services organization the key is to both use that social regulation to move toward productive ends and to generate internal change processes that shift and guide behaviors toward these ends.

Every new member of a relatively bureaucratized human services organization (i.e., an organization possessing the characteristics of specialization, a hierarchy of authority, a system of rules, and impersonality; Blau, 1956) is immediately confronted with the organizational demands and limits on his behavior. The strategies of his own behavior that will ultimately lead to career advancement become clear in a very short period of time. Such strategies have typically involved a redirection of one's own interests to those of the organization (Merton, 1957, pp. 207-244; Kornhauser, 1962; Daniels, 1969). Too often the results have been the dulling of interests and the blunting of potential organizational change processes.

Instant solutions to these problems are not immediately available. Even the more obvious suggestions are filled with difficulties. One of the more prevalent strategies to deal with bureaucratized human services organizations, and one that has achieved some notoriety, is that of decentralizing large and very complex human services organizations. However, few, if any, workable means of decentralizing have been achieved. The most visible recent attempt to decentralize a human service organization has been in the administration of the New York City school system. Not only is there some question whether the decentralized districts (each of which contains a pupil population about the size of the Boston school system) reflect a meaningful decentralization, but as Kristol (1968) suggests, there also are serious questions surrounding a real decentralizing of decision-making power that is commensurate with organizational restructuring. If human service organizations are to be meaningfully decentralized, stronger local authority is necessary. Effective decentralization, Kristol indicates, does not diffuse authority.

Functional strategies of organizational change have not come easily to the human services. The factors of tradition, bureaucracy, and professionalism have combined to render change extremely difficult and problematic. For an assessment of this problem in one area of the human services, the mental hospital, the reader is referred to Goffman (1961) for an overview of the problem and to Hirschowitz (1967; 1969) and Harshbarger (1967) for a view of change strategies and outcomes in single mental hospitals.

New models of human services organizations have, slowly begun to emerge to meet needs created and intensified by rapid population shifts in both urban and rural areas. One of the more popular emergent organizational models in urban areas has been the neighborhood service center, an organization that is made up of interdisciplinary staff members, both professionals and nonprofessionals. But as O'Donnell and Sullivan (1969, p. 10) and Demone (1972), in a review of the literature on neighborhood service centers, have indicated, unless such organizations resolve some very basic problems, numerous organizational malfunctions result. For example, a neighborhood service center must deal with such issues as either emphasizing *(a)* professional direction and administration *or* resident participation and neighborhood control; *(b)* the provision of services *or* social action; *(c)* professional service *or* nonprofessional services; *(d)* information and referral *or* client advocacy and follow-up; *(e)* collaborative and cooperative methods *or* contest and conflict tactics.

The foregoing do not represent all of the issues that confront the neighborhood services center as an organization, and there is no right or wrong way to decide these issues. There are risks and particular constellations of consequences for moving in either direction on any given issue. The point is that role choices must be made by all organizations. They cannot be all things to all people. Moreover, the choices have to be made with a continual view toward the external consequences of these intraorganizational decisions.

ORGANIZATIONAL CHANGE

In large and small ways every organization must attempt to regulate and incorporate into its life the changes in both its external and internal environments. Sometimes this takes the form of building protective barriers in and around an organization so that it is not significantly affected by external changes; at other times, structuring internal organizational relationships so that they continue as they have operated in the past.

As a general rule organizations are more susceptible to change the greater the number of pluralistic interests that directly affect their welfare. A school system, for example, with its single authority, a school board, and a single major source of revenue, local property taxes, is likely to be less open to organizational change than a local mental health organization that survives through a mixture of local, state, and federal funds. Parenthetically, it is worth noting that progress toward desegregation has seemed to have developed a greater impetus in those school districts that have come to rely on federal funds, and hence developed a more pluralistic base of support, than in districts that maintain independent funding sources.

A language of organizational change structure and processes has begun to develop, albeit slowly, and with the softest of data to serve as guides to effective and productive change. Bennis and Slater (1968); and Bennis and Harris (1970) have suggested, at various times, organizational units that are task oriented and temporary in their life and structure. Bennis and Harris (1970) described "organic populism," a form of organizational structure that arises around a problem and a group of concerned, competent persons and that has a relatively temporary organizational life. People in this organization would be differentiated by competence and training, not rank, and leaders would serve primarily linking-pin functions.

Other students of complex organizations, particularly persons who have maintained some long-term association with National Training Laboratories and the T-group movement, such as Bennis, Benne, and Chin, in *The Planning of Change* (1969) and Blake and Mouton (1961) in *The Managerial Grid,* have attempted to articulate strategies of organizational change. Generally, such models of changes as these have involved the adoption of a T-group-oriented model of the change process and integrating it into critical segments of the target organization. In the application of this approach there has been a tendency to focus on the change process per se and a tendency to neglect the long-term consequences of these strategies. As yet it is unclear under what conditions and toward what ends this change strategy is likely to be maximally effective. However, there is virtually universal agreement that it is a powerful change strategy, one that has the potential for generating not only positive organizational changes but also long-term and negative reactive forces within an organization. The latter might be particularly true in human services organizations in which ideologies and professional beliefs are often substituted for empirical outcomes, rendering any evidence of positive organizational changes rather difficult to come by.

A parallel development over the past 15 years has been the growth of the field of systems theory and research as a conceptual framework within which to examine organizational relationships and changes. The field is growing and developing conceptual models but as yet lacks the data base and skills necessary to transpose data across organizations. For an examination of the uses of general system theory in health systems the reader is referred to Sheldon, Baker, and McLaughlin's *Systems and Medical Care* (1970). Von Bertalanffy's (1956) is a more basic text.

It is likely that major, long-term structural changes in organizations and the models that planners envision in designing new organizations will lie in a system's theoretical conception of structural relationships and outcomes. The technologies of change and organizational maintenance will probably lie in approaches reflecting system diagnosis and using those clusters of change tactics best designed to achieve chosen results, controlled by whether goals are short-or long-range and whether the organization views itself as *ad hoc* or permanent. Critical to effective change is an awareness that organizations are made up of people and that their needs must be reflected in the change process.

3. RESOURCES AND THEIR MANAGEMENT

The roles, relationships, and problematic issues that link government, foundations, and voluntary health and welfare agencies are highly complex and in constant flux. Howard (1965, pp. 649-654) describes the latter as follows:

> Questions at issue range from the highly pragmatic—how to secure—*now*—care urgently needed by one group or another—to those involving fundamental philosophies. Among the latter are the nature of the "good society," pluralism, private enterprise, optimal rates of social change and progress, government, bureaucracies (private, whether sectarian or non-sectarian, and governmental), the societal roles of justice, philanthropy and charity, and church-state relationships.

In addition, the historical stereotypes and myths about roles and interorganizational relationships seldom represent contemporary reality.

Some general issues have been decided. Only the government has the financial capacity to raise the level of financial and medical care for larger numbers of low-income people. Which is not to suggest that selected individuals cannot be helped by private enterprise, for veteran, religious, and private social welfare organizations have often given assistance to their members or selected families and individuals at risk; the latter, however, have been the exceptions.

Beyond these fundamental pragmatic issues, organizational functions and roles are becoming increasingly blurred. At best organizations can now be classified as public, quasi public, quasi private, and private. Consider the following:

1. Religious organizations, theoretically separated from the state by constitutional provisions, own tax-deductible property, are the recipients of tax-deductible gifts, and receive government support for specific functions; also, certain of their selected social welfare activities are subsidized by the United Fund.

2. Federal, state, and local governments, in establishing new statutory programs, increasingly suggest that the newly developed organizations secure nonprofit charters.

3. Long-established voluntary organizations, (e.g., the Visiting Nurse Association, receive more than 50% of their operating budgets from Medicare and Medicaid and from contracts with local school and health departments.

The following discussions, entitled Government Organizations, Voluntary Associations, Foundations, and Policy and Politics, are separated in part by sanctions and functions and in part for convenience. Shibboleths notwithstanding, a lack of clarity in making these distinctions is the rule.

GOVERNMENT ORGANIZATIONS

Perhaps most at tension within government is the unclear relation among its various levels; federal, state, county, and local. Issues of philosophy (subsidiarity, centralization and decentralization, and control of various taxing mechanisms) and political power compound the problem. But sheer size, inertia, and the general ineffectiveness of the federal government in delivering direct personal services to people (Veterans' Administration hospitals may be a partial exception) have now led many politicians, public administrators, and political scientists to advocate various forms of federal, non-categorical subsidization of state and local governments. It is reasoned that sheer logistics make it advisable to develop local management and control of programs designed to meet individual, neighborhood, and community needs. As this debate continues and experimentation occurs, new-old struggles between the various levels of government and between local groups wanting community control have developed and intensified.

A side issue, but also a critical one, is the continuing debate between the advocates of categorical and block grants. The revenue-sharing proposals of Presidents Johnson and Nixon represent one position. On the face of it they make considerable sense, but the vigor and heat generated by the opponents suggests that the issues are not simple. Categorical grants can be used to stimulate national priorities and subsidize programs dealing with problems lacking local appeal (e.g., alcoholism). Also, powerful constituencies are usually reflected by each category. A balanced perspective would suggest that both options are needed and that flexibility and timing are the key variables.

Some relevant problems: Large-city mayors want direct access to federal largess, bypassing the traditional federal to state to local formula; the one-man, one-vote Supreme Court ruling is slowly freeing urban areas from the domination of rural areas; town, city, county, and even state boundaries are frequently meaningless as problem-solving areas for human service organizations; efforts to regionalize government flounder even though the failure to develop new and more rational catchment and service areas may make the government increasingly unresponsive to the needs of its citizens; as both the white and black middle class flee the core city for the suburbs, the qualitative differences between central city and suburban schools, and other socializing institutions, are accentuated even further; of the major social institutions, only health, social welfare, and cultural activities are still superior in the urban environment, with the latter primarily serving an affluent user population.

As grants-in-aid and contracting mechanisms have become increasingly common, the issues of quality control

and accountability have become even more important.
Again the question of role functions is at issue. Shall the
federal government do this centrally or via its regional office? Or should this function be delegated to an even
lower level of government; and if so, which level?

As information systems become more sophisticated
and fully exploit computer technology, it is clear that the
vendor will be in a much better position to guarantee
high standards if the vendor can organize to do the job.

One important management control in governmental
human service organizations is in planning and budgeting. With isolated exceptions state and local governments have fallen far behind the federal government in
budgeting technology. Most state and local governments
continue to rely exclusively on object-item budgeting,
and their emphasis is primarily on fiscal control. Budget
bureaus are inadequately staffed, and program planning
is seldom legitimized at either the operating department
or budget department level.

It is true that reform efforts, grants from federal agencies, and even some local appropriations are breathing
new life into antiquated managerial mechanisms, but
considering the pressures on state and local government
and the inadequacies of their responses, time may be running out as alternative structural procedures are sought.

VOLUNTARY ASSOCIATIONS

Voluntary human services organizations are big
business. Billions of dollars are donated every year for
operating and capital purposes. Additional billions are
received as fees, grants, and contracts from individuals,
third-party organizations, government, and foundations.

Standards developed by the National Information Bureau (1968) for philanthropic operations stress responsibility and public trusteeship and suggest specific operational procedures:

1. Board—an active and responsible governing body

serving without compensation, holding regular meetings, and with effective administrative control.

2. Purpose—a legitimate purpose with no avoidable duplication of the work of other sound organizations.

3. Program—reasonable efficiency in program management and reasonable adequacy of resources, both material and personnel.

4. Cooperation—evidence of consultation and cooperation with established agencies in the same or related fields.

5. Ethical promotion. Ethical methods of publicity, promotion, and solicitation of funds.

6. Fund-raising practice—*(a)* No payment of commissions for fund-raising. *(b)* No mailing of unordered tickets or merchandise with a request for money in return. *(c)* No general telephone solicitation of the public.

7. Audit—annual audit, preferably employing the Uniform Accounting Standards and prepared by an independent certified public accountant, showing all support/revenue and expenditures in reasonable detail. New organizations should provide an independent certified public accountant's statement that a proper financial system has been installed.

8. Budget—detailed annual budget, translating program plans into financial terms.

The critical ingredients that differentiate governmental from voluntary organizations are the sponsorship and the trusteeship responsibilities. Typically, the voluntary association offers the individual citizen a greater opportunity to participate in its operation. Citizens are not advisers, but serve policy-making functions in the organization. They, rather than elected and appointed officials, possess the ultimate authority.

At a somewhat less visible level voluntary organizations are not constrained by the increasingly inflexible civil service system, which hampers many governmental organizations. They are potentially much more flexible, although many voluntary associations have failed to capitalize on this difference.

To be effectively differentiated from their governmental peer agencies, a voluntary system must maximize its citizen participation and flexibility. Currently, at a time when individuals are becoming increasingly disenchanted with formal, large, complex, governmental organizations that are seen as distant and inflexible, these are rare opportunities for citizen participation in making voluntary organizations responsive to real needs.

In referring to the health industry, but with equal application to the entire voluntary human service system, the National Commission on Community Health Services (1967, p. 22) commented:

> While the role of the voluntary health agency may appear to have grown less distinct and increasingly difficult to separate from the totality of the health system of the community, this does not mean that its importance has in any way diminished. On the contrary the obligation of the voluntary health agency to the community is even more urgent and compelling than it was in previous years to perform effectively both in its own right and as a genuine partner of the governmental agency. Each has an obligation to be of maximum help to the other in fulfilling their complementary, respective, and joint functions.

It may be that the National Commission has understated the case. Since the 1930s the United States has been dominated by a theory of public administration emanating from the writings and practices of Harry Hopkins. The theory was clean and simple: If an activity was to be a continuing one, the government should operate it. Goods and selected temporary services could be purchased. After almost 40 years of experience this model is now being questioned. Direct human services to people as a function of government have worked well only within certain limited parameters and have seemed unable to deal effectively with the radical changes of post-World War II America. Unfortunately existing services have changed slowly, if at all. Broad-based constituencies and political forces have essentially stalemated the possibility of substantial change. The public administrator is faced with complex and essentially existential conflicts of interests.

Consequently, with increasing frequency consideration is being given to the purchase of services. In this model the government determines priorities, sets standards, and monitors activities conducted for it by service delivery organizations operating on a grant-in-aid, contract, or fee-for-service basis. At this point in time it would appear that organizational flexibility is enhanced and priority change is possible. No longer is the public administrator responsible both to his employees and to the consumers. Role conflict is reduced.

As with any large-scale change in the human services, certain losses may occur. If voluntary agencies do agree to participate in major contract and grant-in-aid arrangements, they abrogate certain freedoms. By definition they must be willing to accept all individuals covered by the agreement. Discrimination is not permitted. Although the latter may not be a problem for many agencies, it may present difficulties for sectarian organizations or agencies established to deal with specific nationality or racial groups.

An additional issue, one which is often debated but seldom resolved, is the proportion of an agency's budget that may be secured from third parties and still not adversely dominate the agency. It is common knowledge in the rehabilitation field that many rehabilitation agencies are unwilling to criticize the state agency, even though it may need such criticisms, and that the specialized agencies are potentially the most appropriate informed bodies. Ecologically, the organization has become over-dependent on a limited resource base. In sometimes not so subtle ways the locus of policy has, via an ecological process, moved outside of the organization.

The voluntary sector has also created an additional form of ecological dependence. That is, through the development of professional overspecialization it has become fragmented, conservative, and increasingly dependent on the value systems of professional organizations.

FOUNDATIONS

According to the Foundation Library Center (1968, p. 55):

> In its purest form a foundation may be defined as a nongovernmental, non-profit corporation or trust, deriving its income from its own endowment managed by its own trustees or directors, and established to make grants for the support of social, educational, charitable, religious, cultural or other activities serving the common welfare. Though not fully meeting specifications of this definition, two other types of organizations are generally recognized by professionals in a broader sense: (1) grant-making organizations; either company-sponsored or family foundations, deriving their funds largely from annual appropriations rather than from endowment; and (2) endowed organizations, called operating foundations, which use most or all of their income to support research or other activities conducted under their own auspices.

Definitional complications are many. Many foundations do not include that term in their title; some others that do use the term are not generally considered foundations. Although in 1970 there were probably more than 10,000 "foundations" in the United States, the bulk of the assets are concentrated in a small group of foundations. Thus, a relatively small number of full-time employees and active board members make policy and allocate the bulk of funds.

These organizations are now divided by law into two types, the private foundation and the public foundation. The private foundation has secured most of its funds from a single individual (e.g., the Ford Foundation) and the public foundation from many individuals (e.g., community foundations). Until the 1969 tax amendments the private foundations were potentially the most creative of all public or private funding organizations. Their constituency was limited to the original supporters (and their families). The philanthropists were limited only by their own inventiveness and the rather limited and unclear law administered by the U.S. Internal Revenue Service. Not in the market for additional donors, they were not required to concern themselves with the attitudes of potential supporters. On the assumption that the broader the base of support the more constrained the organization, the private foundation could be much more flexible than its public counterpart. A fear of Congress (which eventually did act to control their activities), their internal bureaucratic problems, and staff and board differences of opinion have made these organizations much less innovative than possible.

No current discussion of American foundations can take place without mention of Congress's Tax Reform Act of 1969, which contained a section taxing foundations and further regulating their activities.

To agency executives planning to go the foundation route in securing program support, the net result of this law, requiring *(a)* an excise tax on investment income and *(b)* a minimum distribution of income for charitable purposes, may be to create a short-run increase in available funds but a long-run diminution of resources.

Perhaps an even more important consequence of this law is the threat of negative sanctions on foundations, should they exert political influence directly or indirectly. (Financial transactions that might benefit donors or selected other people are also proscribed).

Generally, an immediate result within foundations has been an increase in their tendency to react conservatively to proposals that might have public policy implications. Since most foundations have traditionally been cautious, we can expect to see a further drying up of certain types of venture capital.

Another possibility is suggested by Walsh (1970), who indicates that the foundation staff will now play an increasingly larger role in defining and sometimes generating projects that are to be supported by certain foundations. For smaller foundations that cannot justify full-time well-trained professional managers, joint clearinghouses are being developed to give advice and to act as brokers between worthy applicants and foundations.

POLICY AND POLITICS

Webster defines politics as "the science and art of government; the science dealing with the organization, regulation and administration of a state . . . ;" and "in a bad sense, artful or dishonest management to secure the success of political candidates or parties." For the purposes of this section we are concerned with developing a focus on political roles enacted in human services, organizations, both in and out of those organizations, whether public or private, profit or nonprofit. An administrator, by definition, finds himself in conflict situations or in interactions where he needs the resources and support of persons within and outside of his organization. A majority of administrators' many contacts have political overtones, and administrative favors are given and received. Credits are accumulated and selectively expended.

Mattison (1965) suggests that in understanding this process we start from the perspective of the politician. What are his needs? What would be his model program?

1. The proposed program should be positive, visible, and perceived favorably by the constituents of the politician.

2. The programs should not contain negative components or lead to a tax increase or public disagreement by significant authorities.

3. Favorable effects should be credited, in part at least, to the politician or to his party. Defects, if any, should be the responsibility of the opposition.

4. Programs should be immediately responsive to his constituents. They should be sexy. Drama is preferable. Odds on success should be high.

From the point of view of the elected official, who is subject to re-election every two, four, or six years, such constraints are reasonable. Operating on a limited time-achievement span, subject to the vagaries of voters demanding instant solutions, and responsible to conflicting interests, his preference may be to choose no solution rather than one that may cost money, create dissension, and contain uncertain results. Similar constraints are found in all large organizations that are subject to diverse and pluralistic constituencies. For example, a United Fund with an annual fund-raising campaign operates within these tight constraints. Lacking an ability to compel payment, such as taxes, they can be rejected annually by their givers if their programs are too unpopular or controversial.

Broad-based constituencies are not ordinarily conducive to risk-taking, with low organizational risks being sanctioned, often through silent resistence, not only by those individuals receiving direct services but also by those thousands or millions of people (or their representatives) who subsidize a program. A lack of organizational action and improved service delivery systems that disturb the status quo often has its roots in this broadly defined supportive constituency.

The innovative and creative agency administrator constantly confronts such constraints, tests their limits, and extends or changes them. At the same time he has to be constantly aware of the political realities faced by his major funding sources. A constant source of tension, these fundamental discrepancies, if openly faced and acknowledged, might be reconciled. However, what appears to be an unreasonable demand by an administrator or an unreasonable rejection by the funding source may be justifiable and rational, depending on one's vantage point. Viewing politics as the art of the possible, compromises may be negotiated, but only to the degree that the opposition is understood. Mattison reminds the human services administrator that he, too, is a politician.

Most private and public health and welfare officials formally reject and deny their political roles. An acknowledgement of a political role has been seen as in fundamental conflict with their professional status, although they might ordinarily acknowledge that effective administration requires certain intra- and interorganizational political skills.

Schaefer's study (1962) of public health officers found them denying a political role yet expressing concern over local political pressure or domination. They seemed to yearn for a utopia with public health in but not of government whose determinants would be science and professionalism.

Since public health officers viewed their motives as "right and pure" (compared to politicians), they saw themselves as in key decision-making roles unfettered by political influence. Further, since "the motivations of those with whom he (the public health officer) is dealing were regarded as venal or base, effective negotiation and adjustment may have been impossible." (Schaefer, 1962, p. 326)

What seems so missing, and so necessary, is a view of instrumental political behaviors as both essential and legitimate in the roles of those persons administering or delivering services in human service organizations. Professional ideologies, with their clear and present views of the past, must undergo change. The sense of appropriate reality confrontation and sense of what is legitimate needs a radical updating.

4. THE ELEMENTS
OF PLANNING

Effective community and human services planning in the United States has been an exception not a rule. Our cities have burgeoned, and our rural areas have been drained of their populations. The distribution of our social resources has been unplanned, largely undirected, and lacking in systematic area or regional attempts to create selectively manageable, humane, and productive environments.

In this chapter we begin to delineate some of the basic elements in the planning process, a process that is as complex as it is relevant to the survival of all of us. Although these elements are probably neither unfamiliar nor surprising to most readers, it is important that some consensual base be developed if we are to begin moving toward the use of action-oriented planning to achieve livable communities.

DEFINITIONS

The World Health Organization (1958) defined planning as containing five steps:

1. The collection of information essential for planning.

2. The establishment of objectives.

3. The assessment of barriers and planning for their removal.

4. The appraisal of the apparent and potential resources, funds, personnel, and determination of their interrelationship.

5. The development of a detailed plan of operation, in-

cluding a definite mechanism for continuous evaluation.

Feingold (1969, p. 864) suggests that "Planning . . . is concerned with change, or, in the legislative language, with interference."

Mott (1969, p. 797) describes planning as "an effort on the part of some group or organization to alter the behavior and conditions of other people."

Schools of social work have focused on the teaching of community organization rather than planning, although the definitions overlap. Rothman (1964, p. 24), for example, describes "community organization as geared to the attainment of some social welfare or to the solution of some social welfare problem." The strengthening or rationalizing of existing services, establishing new ones, or changing some negative aspect of an existing community structure, all may be legitimate community organization and planning goals.

To others community organization should not be equated with planning but viewed as one of many methods available to planners. Schools of social work are thus criticized for an overemphasis on a single procedure. Complementing this criticism is the suggestion that process instead of goals are highlighted. For example, Ross (1955, p. 51), a leading scholar of community organization, focuses on "community integration . . . community morale . . . and a spiritual community." The possibility that communities as a heritage of our rural past may not be a meaningful contemporary urban territorial base and that a focus on means, not ends, may divert important energies and thus be counterproductive underscores the weakness of the overemphasis on community organization. The counterargument has been explicated by Pray (1947) who suggests that it is an improper usurpation of role for the social welfare professions to give professional leadership to substantive goals.

Operationally, what is being suggested is that man should have some control over his fate, that he has a right to participate in goal formulation and decision-making regarding the means to ends. The current view focuses on the integration of planning and implementation.

That all too often in human service organizations planners have been the last to be hired and the first to be fired is symptomatic of more serious problems in developing and rationally using resources. Historically, we have not taken planning seriously. As Slater (1970) has suggested, we have tended to be a nation of highly mobile people, a country in which the accepted solution to undesirable living conditions has been to move on. Until recently we had not begun to view ourselves as living in a relatively closed ecological system, one in which there were real limitations to "moving West." We have tended to plan neither our cities nor our human services systems. People have been left to fend for themselves, while those who were able moved to greener pastures, pastures that are now in limited supply and anything but green. In the United States, Slater suggests, everybody thinks that he is the only person in America. That is a hard and harsh reality for a planner; Slater suggests everybody must ultimately realize that he must live with everybody else.

NATURE OF PLANNING

Since change is inevitable and apparently exponential, the wise man usually tries to reduce the elements of luck and chance. Planning implies looking ahead and is based on the premise that events are often related and do not occur singly. It assumes certain cause and effect relations. In the following section we will discuss some of the difficulties in applying the principles of informed planning, for many of the variables are difficult to identify, and people do not always act in their own self interest. Nevertheless, events do occur in some relationship to each other; more than luck, magic, and chance are at work.

In the human services field organized planning occurs

categorically and generically; it can be found in public and private, profit and nonprofit organizations. Categorical planning can be as all encompassing as in the entire field of mental health or as specific as planning for late-adolescent female depressions. It can include the entire medical care system or focus on kidney dialysis and transplantation. Broadly or narrowly conceived, all of these topics would be considered categorical planning, for they do not include other fundamental institutional roles inseparably related to man's good and ill health—his condition as a social animal, his economic and employment status, his housing and education. Only voluntary community health and welfare councils have attempted to view the entire human services network, and even those organizations have usually excluded formal education.

DIMENSIONS OF PLANNING

General and High Impact

A distinction should be made between planning for the general population and especially targeted groups of a high-risk or high-incidence nature. Ordinarily, public bodies are committed to serving an entire eligible population on a case basis, although programs may never actually reach universality. Usually, such delivery arrangements are state supported, sometimes partially subsidized by the federal government. The one major exception is the public health field, which traditionally has concerned itself with primary prevention and high-risk groups.

More recently a new trend, federal to local government, bypassing state government, has stimulated a variety of new programs designed to serve special populations, for example, Model Cities, neighborhood service programs, and Head Start.

Either choice, generic or high impact, has its

advantages and disadvantages. To illustrate, we might briefly note some of the consequences of the more recent federal to local government high-impact programs: New agencies are developed; new actors come into their own; new organizational relationships are established; although the ostensible goal is to reduce duplication and overlapping, the result is usually opposite. Old linkages are violated or ignored; politicians and bureaucrats are often threatened.

Attractive at first, these new arrangements often contain the seeds of their own destruction. As Newman and Demone (1969) have noted, the influence necessary to effectively bypass state governments would have to be amassed by larger and more formidable coalitions than presently exist in the health and welfare system. Each choice is constrained, and an understanding of the alternatives and their implications is a necessary input to effective planning.

Organizational Behaviors

Since it is likely that specific organizations will be asked to alter their programs, success will be enhanced to the degree that the planners are knowledgeable about target organizations. If the goal is to persuade family service agencies to treat more alcoholics or to convince them that they need in-service training in order to deal more effectively with those alcoholics and their families already being seen, a strong familiarity with these organizations is desirable. Further, some sort of reward or inducement mechanism is usually necessary. It could be public recognition, additional funds or staff, and even threats of negative sanctions. It could be as simple as demonstrating to them that they are already treating a number of alcoholics and their families and that they have not been maximally exploiting modern intervention techniques. Whatever suasion is chosen, it should have relevance to the concerned organizations.

Systems Analysis

That systems analysis is no panacea but useful as a tool for dealing with some civil problems is the conclusion of the Denver Research Institute (Gilmore, Ryan & Gould, 1967, p. 1028). Conditional success is dependent on the removal of the numerous obstacles. The Denver Research Institute concludes that while the application of systems theories to community problems (environmental problems, poverty, crime, health, etc.) by defense industries is ". . . unlikely to absorb any great share of total defense resources, . . . its greatest promise is in improving the quality of government administration."

When analyzed, these "new" tools turn out to be those presently used by planners and long evident in planning literature. They have evolved from three different sources: *(a)* the defense systems developed by engineers after World War II, principally as a consequence of the new weapons technology, *(b)* biology, and *(c)* social system theories.

Robert Colbourne (1968), an engineer, then with Mitre Corporation, developed a dozen rules for good systems analysis in a one-page house document:

1. Formulate the problem—it is reasonable to apply 50% of the effort to thinking about the problem. "It's more important to find the 'right' objective than the perfect analytical procedure."
2. Systems analysis should be systems oriented. Although component studies are important. . . . "emphasis should be placed on the simultaneous consideration of all the relevant factors, even if this requires the use of unaided judgment."
3. Alternatives should not be excluded arbitrarily or without analysis.
4. Set forth hypotheses early.
5. The question, not the phenomenae alone, determines the model.
6. The "question" should be kept in mind at all times. The selected model is only a tool, the goal should be foremost.
7. Mathematics and computers although helpful are limited.
8. The enemy is not inert. The opposition must be identi-

fied and its systems, operations and strategies must also be studied and analyzed.

9. The analysis should include uncertainties.
10. Detailed treatment should come late in the study. A rough treatment of many models is better than a careful and detailed treatment of a single model.
11. Suboptimization is necessary or models may become excessively large.
12. Partial analysis is better than no analysis. Inquiry can never be complete.

One concern often ignored by contemporary systems analysts is the frequent need for historical and developmental information. A clearer understanding of the reasons underlying present policy may reveal sources of pressure and key actors not previously identified and reduce error repetition. Since this type of information is seldom available in documents and may even be difficult to obtain by sophisticated interviewers, it may be necessary to immerse oneself in the working of target organizations (Fogelson and Demone, 1969).

Friendship in the Consultative Process

Second in importance to an intimate knowedge of the subject and system is an extended friendship with the many key actors. An open and honest relationship permits a frank exchange on issues, and to the extent that knowedge is shared, major mistakes are less likely to be made. Of course, these same friendships may serve to inhibit change efforts, for the desire to solve problems may be contraindicated by the desire to sustain and enhance personal relationships—a major dilemma in the development of effective human service consultation.

Coordination

One does not easily "bring into common action" (i.e., coordinate) even similar programs. And when the agencies have disparate aims, objectives, skills, and beliefs, the process is compounded. Yet both public and voluntary organizations are increasingly claiming for themselves a coordinative, collaborative, and linkage role.

Whatever the circumstances and time, acknowledgement of a coordinative function stems from two factors: *(a)* pluralism and *(b)* the absence of a formal central administrative authority.

Faced with the extraordinarily complex array of interests and organizations, especially in newly developed fields of interest (e.g., drug programs in the early 1970s), the customary choice among intervention strategies will be coordination. The assumption is that if agencies meet and talk together about common interests, they will be both less parochial and more likely to cooperate, possibly even to collaborate. Although coordination is useful, even vital at times, it is important that planning not stop with coordination. It is a beginning, a means, not an end in itself.

Involvement

A powerful technique is involvement. Even resistant individuals committed to the status quo may sometimes be persuaded to consider alternatives when they are consulted and participate as a major force in the process. A more cynical view would describe involvement as co-optation.

Consumer Participation

Belief in consumer participation, an essential ingredient of a democracy via the ballot box, and occasionally through public advisory committees, and integral to the voluntary association through policy-making boards of trustees, has now become an act of faith widely advocated and built into most contemporary federal and state statutes. As with all panaceas it will fail to bring about the desired ends, frustrating the true believers but likely producing some lesser but still important results. If we are to assume that all large complex organizations have a tendency to close in on themselves and to prefer the reactive to the proactive, any institutional mechanisms that will help to counteract these tendencies are beneficial in allowing for another countervailing force to technocracy.

Planners, too, will have their consumer participants and the same exaggerated promises and resistances. If consumers are involved as "representatives" of the population of users, they will surely fail to live up to expectations. They have not been chosen randomly, they are not "representative." At best, they represent themselves. If a representative sample of opinion is wanted, an appropriately designed household survey is better. If consumer representation is selected to broaden the base of participants, to challenge the status quo, and to contribute case material, then this method will be productive. Most importantly, it is eventually the consumer who makes the final judgment about what kinds of services are desired, how they are to be delivered, their form, and the setting (Hochbaum, 1969).

Coalitions

Two complementary principles are at work in the current emphasis on coalition planning. First is the acknowledgement that the pluralistic nature of our society usually requires the cooperation of a wide variety of organizations and individuals if planning is to succeed. An equally important point is that coalitions and alliances formed at various stages in the planning process are necessarily flexible and subject to change. As the nature of the suggested changes becomes more specific, allies tend to become more discriminating in their support (Fogelson & Demone, 1969).

Leadership

In addition to formally ascribed leaders, in most complex environments informal leaders also develop. The latter may not possess the influence or power to bring about major change against opposition, but they often possess veto power in issues related to their spheres of interest.

Further, informally achieved leadership is not highly stable but is constantly shifting, depending on the issue under consideration, with the internal system dynamics being critical variables. Nevertheless, identification of issue leaders is critical if change is to be successful.

Politics: Power and Influence

Despite a current mythology that posits power among individuals and organizations, it seldom exists in the simplistic terms expounded by its critics. Power implies the capacity to determine outcome, a capacity seldom found in our pluralistic society.

Many individuals and groups have influence, especially the capacity to veto undesired recommendations. We do not suggest that power and influence are not important. In fact, identification, recognition, and working with such individuals and groups is vital for success. We merely deplore many current simplistic explanations. Most groups and individuals with influence or power use their capacity sparingly. Further, such sanction capacity varies by issue and time. For the most part such strength is used to defend or promote private interests, not for the public good. Exceptions from the "sparing-use criteria" are those groups whose functions include the formal use of influence. Included would be political parties, organized labor, chambers of commerce, taxpayers' associations, and the League of Women Voters. This does not imply that these and similar groups use their strength indiscriminately but that their interests are broad and they are expected to speak out on a variety of issues.

The world of real power relationships requires extraordinary political sophistication on the part of planners

Knowledge of the political dynamics of planners would (also) contribute to development of more realistic theory to

guide practice, and to theory that reconciles the rational
elements of the current models with relevant political factors (Mott, 1969, p. 802).

Reinforcing this premise, Mott (1969, p. 802) goes even
further:

> It is difficult to see how planning can be made more effec-
> tive, regardless of improvements in planning technologies,
> data collection, and analysis, without explicit recognition
> of the functions of power, and thus of politics, in making de-
> cisions that involve conflicting values and interests.

Incremental Planning

It is usually necessary to accept incremental planning
to achieve goals over a period of time. Both administrator and planner must avoid rigidity as to the amount and
form of these incremental changes. An historical perspective is particularly useful to their egos, for change is a
continuing process often occurring in modest steps. Such
a perspective may also help community groups develop
an historical sense of gains.

Estimating Costs

The determination of costs is a critical component of effective planning. This type of question will be uppermost
in the minds of most sanctioning bodies. In a two-page
statement developed for the Massachusetts Vocational
Rehabilitation Planning Project in 1967, Newman suggested that of the four options:— (a) ignore; (b) conscious-
ly reject as a planning responsibility; (c) treat as a staff
responsibility after all the basic work has been done; and
(d) integrate cost issues throughout the planning process—the latter is the most effective. He also suggests
that if you cannot or do not cost out a proposal, then it is
not a recommendation but a statement of principle or
philosophy and that if you cannot cost the recommendation, do not expect implementation.

Future Planning

By definition, all planning is future oriented. But a special future view has developed in recent years. Almost faddish now, dozens of groups are involved in futurism. A World Future Society has been established, international meetings are held, and a journal exists. The United Nations now includes a future planning unit.

Kopkind (1967) cities some comments on the subject: A *Fortune* editor—"the greatest advance in the art of government (in) nearly a hundred years." Daniel Patrick Moynihan—"It is an idea whose time is coming." Michael Harrington—"one of the most radical suggestions put forth by a responsible body in our recent history." To Tom Hayden, it is "a new barbarism." At the moment opinions are not polarized according to any identifiable ideology, although strong opinions are common.

For the purposes of this section we shall focus on certain implications for planners. The final chapter of this monograph will examine some of the more general substantive issues.

Because the art is so new, agreed-upon definitions are not yet available, but some tentative efforts at clarification are possible.

> . . . it is a collection of vaguely related, political and intellectual happenings that have to do with new ways to analyze, anticipate and control the social environment. Involved are elements of old-fashioned central planning and new-fangled futurism; but the participants are more than planners and less than utopians. . . . They dream of using social science instead of presure politics to solve the nation's problems. (Kopkind, 1967, p. 19)

One point is clear: The maximum use of modern and future technology is included in future planning—soft ware and hardware. Donald Michael (1967) lists a number of existing social engineering technologies already available: systems analysis, planning-program-budgeting systems; economic control mechanisms; the human engineering of weapon systems; the application of new managerial theories, and the use of behavioral science research in urban design. Additional technologies include new research on the relation between human behavior and physical structure; the growing application of operational-evaluation research; games theories; model building; and simulation. Raymond Bauer and Bertram Gross have been working intensively on social goals and social indicators. The latter would parallel the economic indicators now used so successfully by all industrialized nations.

Underlying many of these advances is the latest generation of computers. The computer allows the future planners to store large amounts of data, extrapolate, build models, simulate experiments, and test hypotheses. For the first time complex models, which more nearly resemble what goes on in real life, are possible.

The key question, as yet unanswered by the future planners, is: Who poses the questions to be answered?

5. DEVELOPING OPERATIONAL PLANS

To the administrator or planner, developing operational plans means confronting the social, political, and economic facts of life. It means developing a conceptual framework in which the planner or planning group can assess its efforts and propose directions in the light of regarding what is salient and what is feasible must be made. Alternatives have to be examined in terms of short- and long-term gains and costs.

In the development of operational plans a planner or a planning group must continually remind themselves of the sometimes overlooked fact that they may influence the lives of many people if their plans are implemented. Through the establishment of policies, priorities, and resource allocations they are placing limits on the possible. Conditions are being created within which some behaviors and not others can and will occur. Shall such specific programs as drug abuse and alcoholism be given priority over more general programs such as those of community mental health in the relative allocation of resources? Shall a community sell bonds for the purpose of constructing low-cost housing or for the purpose of a more adequate human service agency or hospital facility?

Developing operational plans means engaging in the operations that actively place limits on some kinds of human interactions and facilitate other kinds of interaction and community development. Hopefully, what is facilitated moves in directions that best meet the salient needs of a community.

Operational plans do not come easily. As noted in the previous chapter, many mixed, varied, and often conflicting interests must be taken into account. Planners must work with both fantasy and reality. Their idealism may spur them on, but their knowledge of practical politics will make them successful.

HEALTH PLANNING HISTORY

The capacity to learn from previous generations and to improve the quality of planning helps to distinguish *homo sapiens* from animals. Thus Man has always planned. To suggest the evolution of form and structure, we will highlight the American health planning field in the twentieth century.

Health planning as a discrete entity can essentially be traced through three separate but overlapping subsystems. One theme reflects the 50-year history of voluntary health and welfare planning councils, with emphasis on coordination and community organization. Next, perhaps, was the emphasis on hospital beds and construction beginning in the 1930s. Last was the physical. City planners in the last decade or so began to emphasize the individual in his environment. Structurally, four steps, not necessarily sequential, can be identified. Health divisions or councils were formed as integral components of voluntary health and welfare councils. Subsequently, sometimes as a spin-off and sometimes independently, hospital councils were established. At first they were envisaged as broad-based hospital facility-planning organizations, but for the most part they became federated trade associations representing hospital administrators and some trustees. Next, stimulated by the federal Hill-Burton Construction Act new hospital councils were developed as quasi-public facility-planning organizations.

During the 1960s a series of experiments in *ad hoc* state planning occurred in mental health, retardation, and rehabilitation. Essentially fully supported by the federal government, grants-in-aid were made to state-designated authorities. On the whole these intensive short-term efforts (usually two years) were surprisingly productive, expecially mental health and retardation. The latter two were closely tied to federal construction and staffing grants and essentially offered rewards for selected efforts. The rehabilitation planning effort (as with comprehensive health planning, to be discussed next), more process oriented than goal oriented, have yet to be as productive.

And finally, the late 1960's saw the passage by Congress of the Partnership for Health Act and the Regional Medical Program. As a consequence new quasi-public comprehensive health planning agencies have generally replaced the facility planning organizations.

In some areas all forms of "health planning" still exist, although in an unclear and stressful relation. The 1970s should shake down roles more clearly.

Despite the long-standing form and structure, until recently financial support and sanctions were very limited.

The principal financial base had been the United Way movement and its predecessor organization, although in the 1960s the hospital councils began to be self-supporting. State and local governments, as has been their wont, generally disdained planning and offered neither financial nor moral support, although some health officers and their aides participated as individuals. (In a few states the Hill-Burton Construction Act was used by state health departments to stimulate some rationality in hospital construction.)

At the point that federal funds became available and some teeth were put into the planning effort, new, independent, free-standing organizations were developed on the premise that the previously undermanned, under-financed, and limited-sanctioned agencies had not been successful. It has been suggested that the use of the existing health-planning apparatus that had developed strong community links and support related to the larger social welfare system would threaten the complete dependence on the federal counterpart organization. It was safer for the bureaucracy to establish a new system.

At this point certain trends are obvious. State government is nominally involved via 314A Comprehensive Health Planning agencies, but they have been assigned limited powers and limited budgets. If the states wish to assume a more significant role, they will find it necessary to appropriate larger sums directly from their own budgets, expand the A agencies' influence by statutory and regulatory charges, and remove it from the control of state-operating agencies.

Except on paper, and with some singular exceptions, local governments have been effectively bypassed.

The regional 314B agencies, although statutorily comprehensive, have been principally concerned with facilities, primarily hospitals. It is likely that this interest will expand to include health services, although human services, broadly conceived, and environmental planning will probably continue to receive short shrift. Trends already evident also suggest that state governments will assign certain statutory review responsibilities to the 314B agencies, thus confounding further their confused voluntary-public status. It is reasonable to expect that increased state control over the B agencies will follow the latter's increased responsibility. At the moment, the private sector, especially general hospitals, still dominates the B agencies. Consumers are principally represented by the business, financial, and legal interests and the "professional poor."

A separate effort directed principally to heart, cancer, stroke, and kidney disease—the Regional Medical Program (RMP),—is an effort to regionalize facilities and providers to offer improved services. Essentially controlled by the nation's medical schools, RMP has concentrated on continuing education of health professionals, formalizing linkages between teaching and community hospitals and individual physicians, and the support of some new services. It suffers the same tensions and strains as comprehensive health planning, although its more limited charge makes it currently more viable.

Certainly, these models are temporary, although comprehensive health planning in any form is unlikely in the near future. We know too little, and it is too threatening. Pluralism, marketplace decisions, and incrementalism will undoubtedly remain with us, and at this point in time such an arrangement is probably advisable.

An interesting and important side effect is that large state departments (especially Public Health, Mental Health, Welfare and Rehabilitation) are for the first time in most states developing a planning competence of their own, if only to defend their own interests. At the state level this may be the most significant development of the 1970s.

HEALTH CARE PLANNING

In developing operational plans for health care, the planner must deal with established community interest groups that are equal in their power and complexity to those groups encountered in comprehensive urban planning. It does the planner little good to rail against the medical establishment; it is equally dysfunctional for him to behave as if that establishment did not exist or that it cannot be changed.

As noted in our historical analysis, comprehensive health care planning has not been an integral part of the American medical scene, although there has been some limited health care planning. Historically, the planning that has occurred has usually been based on assumptions suggesting the long-term continuation of the individual practitioner, fee-based medical delivery system. Only recently has there been a realization of the very serious limitations on both the services that can be provided and the target populations that can be reached through the use of this model. Daniel Schorr's *Don't Get Sick in America* (1969) provides a very thorough descriptive analysis of these problems.

For the planner concerned with comprehensive health care, the preceding should mean an increase in the power of his position. National Health Insurance may be only a few years away; comprehensive health planning is already legislatively enacted and beginning to test its political muscles. The planning of health services is being seen increasingly as a community problem, not a problem that is the exclusive province of a select group of medical practitioners or hospital administrators.

An effective health care planner must combine in his talents the long-range views of a sophisticated theoretical-conceptual orientation and an accurate short-term perception of present political reality; too often in the past offices of planning have been characteristically one of these or the other. That is, either they operated a "wishful thinking" model of planning, one that was relatively conceptually advanced but detached from political reality, or they operated in a "political reality" model, one that was effective in short-term gains but lacked long-term concepts and direction.

Presently, there exists a greater impetus for change in health care delivery systems than at any time in the recent past. The inadequacies of traditional models of service delivery have generated forces for change both inside and outside professional health organizations. It is in everyone's best interest that health care systems change and begin to truly serve the needs of a total population. However, whether the plans that are developed focus on more and larger medical schools and on an attempt to meet the current health crisis through simply producing more physicians or whether these plans realize the critical need to develop alternative models of service delivery will probably be the major issue confronting the health planner at the outset of his operational efforts. Although it can be statistically demonstrated that producing more physicians who will practice in existing solo practitioner models of service delivery will place us farther and farther behind in meeting critical health needs, planning and developing alternative models of health care will be anything but easy.

The classic planning model, (Aronson, 1964) includes the following steps to strengthen the health care planner's position: *(a)* developing an advisory planning group that represents political power in a community; a group that is politically sensitive to community needs; *(b)* developing some instrument of survey research that puts together an overview of existing facilities and resources with an overview of community needs; *(c)* the development and assessment of new models of health delivery, with these designed to move the existing system in the direction of greater comprehensiveness; also included would be the placing of priorities for resource allocation regarding new facilities and program development, thus providing an opportunity to reward potentially more effective delivery systems; and *(d)* developing plans for action. It cannot be assumed that a community will rationally contemplate alternative models and act in its own best interest. Unfortunately, communities that are in greatest need of more effective health delivery systems are likely to be those communities that are most disorganized and anomic. Consequently, the planning group must include in their design a variety of means of political action that will help to ensure a follow-through on their efforts. Not to make this latter step a critical part of the planning group's actions would be to risk inaction, atrophy, and the creation of just one more interesting idea that is collecting dust on a shelf.

Also, unfortunately, if a health care or any other planning group is unsuccessful, it most likely will be due to the lack of effective implementation strategy and capacity. It is this oversight that all planning groups are most likely to commit; it is also the oversight that is most difficult to avoid.

ENVIRONMENTAL HEALTH PLANNING

Architect Erro Sarrinen often suggested that if any element of design or architecture was to be understood, it had to be seen in the context of the next larger unit. That is, an article of furniture could only be understood in the context of the room; a room only understood in the context of other rooms and their joining corridors; a house or building, in turn, had to be viewed in relationship to the larger surrounding factors in the environment, such as terrain and topography, other buildings, etc.

Using the language of systems analysis, similar approaches are being applied to areas of planning. For example, effective antitoxin delivery systems to combat mercury and lead poisoning make little sense if steps are not taken to curb the frequency and probability of these forms of poisoning. Ultimately, major environmental variables must be brought under control if we are to plan for a relatively healthy society.

Some historians have suggested that the decline of the Roman Empire was not due to such socioeconomic factors as affluence, taxation, increased leisure time, and changed child-rearing practices. Rather, the upper classes of Roman society literally poisoned themselves to death through their routine use of lead drinking containers. Similarly, one might argue that through a variety of means, generally much more complex and imaginative than those used by the Romans, we are committing chemical suicide.

Compounding these ecological problems is that across the United States local and county public health offices have tended to lack the political power and clout that might have lead to some effective environmental controls. Ecologically, such a condition has probably been in the best economic interests of special interest groups, such as the chemicals and housing industries, as well as the fee-based medical practitioner. Through what is an unintentional and unorganized coalition of public and private interests, public health departments have been able to render little more than advice and relatively innocuous programs, and then only after protracted political warfare.

Further compounding the problems of environmental health is the systematic nature of environmental problems. The American Public Health Association (1968,

p. 358) has pointed this out in their suggestion that:

> if it is decided to reduce air pollution by prohibiting apartment house incineration, the storage of the wastes pending their collection may create problems of rodent and insect infestation, while collection services must be increased over and above those formerly required for the incinerator residue. Disposal will also create additional problems. . . .

At this point in time the Federal Environmental Protection Agency is only beginning to test its strength. National and local concerned citizens' groups are beginning to develop programs for environmental ecological controls but as yet have not significantly reduced the release of potentially harmful pollutants. Only a few industries have begun to generate even minor self-regulating procedures. Whether or not these efforts can be coordinated and effectively brought to bear on the significant environmental health problems facing the United States *before* these problems reach crisis proportions is open to question. It is a major task that confronts the health planner concerned with environmental planning.

MENTAL HEALTH PLANNING

For over a decade various segments of the mental health professions have been actively struggling to free themselves from their historical orientations and major concerns with individual pathology and treatment. Since the report of the Joint Commission on Mental Health (Gurin, Veroff, & Feld, 1961), these efforts have gradually and continually increased.

The passage of the 1963 Community Mental Health Centers Act made available modest amounts of federal resources to facilitate this effort. Basically, it was an enactment of the joint commission's recommendations that intervention in mental health problems occur early and as close as possible to the patient's home community. With the development and deployment of these resources, strategies were generated to facilitate mental health programs that focused on intervention at the level of the community rather than at the more traditional level of the individual patient. Disease models of mental illness began to share with biosocial models of family and community problems.

Among those mental health professionals who have vacated their one-to-one therapy and mental hospital orientations, a considerable amount of first-hand knowledge has been generated regarding how operational mental health plans might be effectively developed and implemented. Demone, Spivack, and McGrath (1966), Fogelson and Demone (1969), Freed, Schroder, and Baker (1970), and Freed and Miller (1971) have provided case studies of many of the political-professional problems that are generated when mental healthers engage in community action.

Such case studies as these suggest three primary sources of problems that are likely to confront the mental health planner. First is the resistance of the target community. Mental health or any other kind of human service programs cannot be delivered as a *fait accompli*. No matter how good the programs, the probability of their being unsuccessful, even rejected outright by the community, are increased to the extent that community members have not played an active role in the development of the program. While this may seem an overly simplistic observation, and certainly nothing new after the turmoil of the late 1960s, it remains a serious problem for some mental health professionals and planners. They continue to assault and insult communities through a lack of genuine regard for community needs and, most importantly, a willingness to share influence with their communities. Many good words and thoughts have been expressed about this problem; it is something that mental health professionals "know." Yet communities continue to have to fight for a voice in mental health planning and programming.

The formula $e = f(q)(a)$ symbolically expresses this

problem. In this formula e refers to effectiveness of programs, f to a mathematical function, q to program quality, and a to community acceptance of these programs. Thus, if the program is of poor quality but highly accepted, or if the program is of high quality but is not accepted, the effectiveness is roughly the same. The equation has been reduced to an outcome of zero through the inclusion of a zero as a multiplier. The program will not function effectively.

A second major problem area is the resistance of established mental health groups in communities in which new community mental health programs are being proposed. Combinations of medical-psychiatric, welfare, and other interests may actively resist the development of these programs and facilities. Although the issues tend to become abstract and philosophical; (e.g., socialized medicine, the uses of nonprofessionals, etc.) at the core of the problem usually lies a displacement of political-economic interests. And, realistically, it is probable that individual psychiatrists in a community *are* likely to find that their political positions have been diminished by the development of a community mental health center. (Their practice may be enlarged as their individual influence decreases.) However, it is also possible that a community mental health center will act in their, as well as the community's, best interests. The two are not necessarily mutually exclusive.

In part the problem is also conceptual. If the disciples of community mental health advocate a monopolistic or oligopolistic model, they are both denying the realities of our pluralistic society and actively inviting major resistance. Community mental health does not require the building of another complex bureaucracy.

Finally, a third set of problems confront the mental health planner from inside the community mental health professions themselves. As Roland Warren (1969) has so perceptively described it, mental health professionals, having made a commitment to a community approach to mental health problems, do not really know what to do with themselves. Warren likens urban communities and some of their resident human service professionals to the old Broadway hit *Hellzapoppin,* a play filled with spontaniety, involvement, and wit that exploded beyond the confines of the stage into the audience. However, Warren suggests that the mental health professionals seem to bear more of a resemblance to Hamlet rather than the characters in *Hellzapoppin,* and, like Hamlet, having found themselves in the midst of *Hellzapoppin's* communities' change and conflict, wonder whether "To be, or not to be . . .."

FACILITIES PLANNING

In the final analysis the development of a human services program will often lead to some form of facilities planning either through the development of new facilities or the modification of existing ones. For better or worse we tend to link our programs to bricks and mortar. Such an approach has had the obvious asset of providing a new territorial base from which programs can be developed and protected but has also carried the liabilities of potential isolation, inflexibility, and great expense.

To the planner of facilities for the human services, facilities planning should be seen as an outcome of program development not the structure within which major programs will be generated. The questions of what facilities will be needed, where, and at what cost should be feasible resultants of program design and innovation. Unfortunately, in the past we have too often reversed this relationship. We have found ourselves with already constructed facilities that place enormously restrictive parameters on the nature of the programming that is possible within their confines.

The core issues in facilities planning are those of programs and priorities. For purposes of the present discussion it might be assumed that these have been worked through, although as the reader may know only too well, it can never be safely assumed that these are closed issues.

In developing plans for facilities, Spivack and Demone (1970) provided the following model; a model with areas of concern that should be coordinated and supervised by the planner in the order listed:

I. Comprehensive and long-range planning.
  1. Budgetary planning.
  2. Legislative involvement.
II. Project planning.
  1. Communications and community organization.
  2. Statewide site location studies.
  3. Site selection.
  4. Complete administration of architect selection procedures.
  5. Architectural contract administration, management. Consultation to and free dialogue with architects and their local clients (staff of future facility) during all phases of architectural work.
  6. Architectural programming research.
  7. Site planning studies.
  8. Schematic drawings.
  9. Preliminary design studies.
  10. Final design drawings.
  11. Working drawings.
  12. Review and release of construction contracts and schedules.
  13. Construction and on-site design modifications.
  14. Establishment of maintenance standards, schedules and procedures, and their supervision.
III. Evaluative research review and feedback.
  1. Continued research.
  2. Review and feedback.

The use of this model will not ensure effective facilities planning; however, it will prevent some of the more serious errors and provide a set of guidelines and bench marks against which the facilities-planning process can be monitored.

URBAN PLANNING AND HUMAN SERVICES

Historically, human services organizations have been only peripherally involved, if at all, in the processes of urban (city) planning. An exception to this would be our schools, a form of human services that has usually been given a site location in the early development of communities. Even this inclusion has been limited. Schools, conceptually, have rarely been seen in terms of their full potential in a community. Rather, they have been regarded as a physical facility, one in which a known, constricted, and predictable socialization process is expected to take place. The full potential of schools as a major community resource and the multiple uses of school facilities have rarely been taken into account in physical planning.

Conceptually, the plans for urban areas have been narrow, limited, and only marginally successful. However, as Logue indicates in his forthright and occasionally humorous "The power of negative thinking," (1969) the planning and execution of effective community and human services development is a realistic, practical possibility, but it demands more than we have given it up to now.

Perhaps as indicative of the limited views of human services is that human services organizations have tended to emerge *after* the development of urban problems rather than in a preventive framework. Community models for human services development seem to have paralleled the use of the fire department from which firemen are called to extinguish a blaze. Too often human services organizations have been developed and activated after the fact, when the best that might be done is to minimize damage.

Ardell (1969) has noted that a number of recent legislative acts may operate to change this situation. The Comprehensive Health Planning and Public Health Service Amendments of 1966 asked for health planning that included both long- and short-range comprehensive health plans and service delivery systems. Similarly, model cities, model neighborhood development legislation, and the Safe Streets Act place the human services in a somewhat better position to influence urban planning.

These legislative acts theoretically provided human service organizations with resources to be allocated;

hence, contingencies can be placed on the allocation of resources in such a way that effective multilevel planning must occur before resources will be allocated. Thus, in order for there to be urban, core-city redevelopment, there must be certain networks of human services that are planned. Without these plans the physical changes in a community's bricks and mortar cannot occur. Similarly, before new hospitals are to be built in suburban areas, existing and planned comprehensive networks of inpatient treatment facilities must be examined for that geographic area. It may be that other facilities, such as outpatient clinics, would more effectively meet community needs.

The preceding represent simple questions with very complex answers and assume implementation of legislative intent. They have to do with expenditures of billions of dollars. Until recently, the human service professional or the human services planner found himself excluded from the urban planning process. There was no effective way for him to intervene in plans for the inner city, the suburbs, or whatever. Aside from his skills he lacked resources with which he could effectively barter. Recent legislation suggests that changes might be under way. How effective planners are in the bargaining process and how well they might use these resources is still an open question.

Rand (1969) makes the simple but powerful observation that the new towns of tomorrow are being designed today. The constraints under which we may live are being developed now. Tomorrow will be too late to question today's assumptions.

6. POLICIES, ACCOUNTABILITY, AND SOCIAL CHANGE

A number of factors combine to render human services organizations less open to changes in policies and resource allocations than might be true in equal-size profit-making business organizations. For one, most human service organizations have become relatively bureaucratized, with various organizational pressures operating to continue, largely unchanged, intraorganizational routines. Another factor has been the tendency for these organizations to become professionalized through the selective hiring and retention of employees who meet certain criteria in their training and experience. Generally, these criteria have been developed and maintained by various professions, such as associations of social workers, physicians, psychologists, rehabilitation counsellors, etc., independently of the concerns of any particular human services organization or community.

A third factor giving rise to long-term organizational inertia has been the relative independence of human services organizations in their patterns of funding. Public schools, hospitals, social welfare organizations, and state mental hospitals have not been constrained by profit-making responsibilities. Criteria other than profit are applied to determine success, such as caseload, number of patients, and number of persons receiving particular kinds of training. These outcomes have typically been assessed in terms of their social utility by respective funding organizations, such as legislatures, city councils, or United Funds. Barring major and obvious discrepancies between the cost of a human services organization

213

and its assessed social utility, that organization will continue to operate with only minor changes in its internal roles and external relationships.

These factors have, historically, equipped human services organizations to survive and grow remarkably well in environments that have been relatively stable and predictable. And as long as the environment remained relatively low in its turbulent qualities, the cost of these organizations were generally commensurate with their social utility.

However, it would be inaccurate to describe the environments in which human service organizations must survive in the United States today as stable and predictable. Rather, as noted earlier, these environments, particularly in urbanized areas, might be more accurately described as high in environmental turbulence (Emery & Trist, 1965). High levels of stress are being placed on the adaptive abilities and resources of human services organizations, organizations that have too often in the past behaved like Procrustus, requiring that their clientele design their problems to suit the organization's capabilities.

The present chapter is concerned with adaptation and change in human service organizations. Its focus will be on the locus of policy-making and resource allocation, models of social change and change agents, and the nature of the change strategy. The purpose of this chapter is to provide an overview of strategies that are likely both to increase a human services organization's responsiveness to client or environmental needs and to maximize the effectiveness of their interventions.

THE LOCUS OF POLICY-MAKING AND RESOURCE ALLOCATIONS

Virtually every human services organization is directly accountable to some form of superordinate organization known as a board of trustees or directors, a council, or some similar title (ultimately the executive and legislative branches in government.) The formal function of these superordinate bodies is twofold: *(a)* to monitor, however nominally, the routine activities of the organization and *(b)* to establish major organizational policies and approve the allocation of the organization's resources.

In order to successfully perform these two formal functions, however, other perhaps more important informal functions must be effectively carried out. For example, in formally monitoring the activities of an organization, little can be gleaned from formal accounting procedures regarding where staff spend their work days, although this information may be valuable in developing some overall view of how and where resources are being expended. A more important informal activity for a board member is his interaction with staff members, often during off-duty hours.

Another major informal activity is the degree to which a board serves to link both the community's power structure and that organization's client community. The lines of communication must run in both of these directions if the organization is both to survive and maintain its relevence to community problems.

Board members who are members of what might be loosely termed a community power structure are potentially invaluable in negotiating on behalf of an organization vis-à-vis superordinate bodies (e.g., city councils, state legislatures, federal review boards, United Way budget committees) that control major resources. An organization that lacks board members who can and will perform this vital ecological function is likely to find itself deficient in survival resources, beginning to atrophy, and ultimately dying.

Although this adaptive strategy has a number of functional properties in terms of an organization's political and economic growth and survival, it has often resulted in human services organizations becoming more responsive to funding agencies than to client communities. It has become almost commonplace to hear of human services organizations charged with having grown away from, or being irrelevant to, the needs of their client communities.

Although there have been many attempts to deal with this problem through developing better community relationships, conducting relatively accurate surveys of needs, etc., in the final analysis the problem has become one of the degree to which communities are to share in establishing policy and allocating resources in these organizations. The local organizations that have emerged through Office of Economic Opportunity funds have been leaders in this effort, although their attempts to develop "maximum feasible participation" among the poor in their programs and organizational development have become controversial and problematic, at the very least.

Two major issues have emerged from the above: *(a)* Shall community representatives share in the development of policies and programs? *(b)* If so, at what level shall the sharing of power occur? In the confusion resulting from these issues, client power in policy-making has been seen as a means of legitimizing influence in the execution of policy. Board members often become agents of interference in the daily activities of the organization or at best have begun to monitor daily organizational activities with considerable diligence, persistence, and not so subtle hints that their observations are likely to influence their decisions as board members.

In other situations, such as the subject of a case study by Gilbert (1969), in which citizens and professionals clashed in Pittsburgh's community action program, citizens' groups have been primarily influential in dealing with nonbasic issues confronting the organization.

Beck (1969) has suggested that "community control" is a distraction not an answer to the problem of making agencies responsive to their client communities. Citing Etzioni's use of "inauthenticity," Beck suggests that human service organizations that respond to confrontations with poor or minority groups by placing some of these persons on policy-making boards may be giving a false response to a real need. The major problem is that of the distribution of wealth; a minor and perhaps related problem is the immediate one of service delivery.

Although having representative members of the client community in policy-making bodies may be a worthwhile end, it should be seen realistically for what it is—an attempt to improve the service delivery system, a system that may already be operating under conditions of inadequate staffing and financing. Placing community members on the policy board may simply raise expectations in the community and not lead to meaningful changes in community life.

A policy-making and resource allocating board should represent both the community it serves and the community from which it receives resources. Very often these are two mutually exclusive groups. Human services organizations in urban ghetto or Appalachian communities receive finances and legitimizing political sanctions from those parts of society that have wealth and political power to give. By and large these are not the organization's clients. In turn, a human services organization must be relevant to the needs of the community it serves. Through the use of what Saul Alinsky terms "native leadership" (1945) or indigenous community leadership, organizations that truly serve "the people" can be shaped.

In short, that is what the board of a human services organization is about. Political representatives from resource providers and persons in need form a group that must compose and orchestrate a score known as organizational policies. To do this effectively, they must be highly integrated and in touch with each other, as well as with the groups that they represent. A primary task of the human services organization's leadership is to facilitate this integration. And it is in their best interest to do so; ultimately, they must play the composition and face the critics.

SOCIAL CHANGE: CHANGE
AGENTS AND STRATEGIES

Social change has become a major and pervasive contemporary problem. People are finding themselves both deeply involved in it and overwhelmed by it. Human services organizations are being called on to deal with many of the dysfunctional, often crisis-ridden outcomes of social and technological change, as well as to intervene in the change process itself. Very often staff in these organizations have found themselves simultaneously trying to deal not only with change processes and their outcomes but also attempting to generate models of the change process that might give them a means of intellectually grasping and exercising some control over the flow of events.

An immediate problem that any human services organization must face in developing policies and programs aimed at social change is that of *why* they are about *what* they are about. That is, what is the purposive nature of their proposals? Where should it take both the organization and the client community? As Rein and Miller (1966) have asked, what are the potential assets, liabilities, targets, and yardsticks of success?

Moreover, what is the framework in which the change program is being developed? Moynihan (1966) has suggested that powerful differences arise in programs depending on whether they are conceptualized within a "bureau of the budget concept," with efficiency the guiding principle; an "Alinsky concept," with conflict the guiding principle; a "Peace Corps concept," with provision of services of major importance; or a "Task force concept," in which the primary concern is that of political effectiveness.

Freidmann (1969) has pointed to an additional problem in conceptualizing social change programs, which, if unresolved, tends to create a basic ambivalence in the host organization, (i.e., whether the emerging programs are seen by the host organization as system maintaining or system transforming.) Too often, in efforts to avoid this fundamental policy conflict, programs that are actually system maintaining are marketed as system transforming to client groups. Conversely, there is a tendency to market system-transforming programs to resource-providing groups as programs of system maintenance. Finally, there is a tendency for organizations not to really attack this problem in their internal relationships. As might be expected, the outcome is one of increased levels of confusion and conflict both within the organization and in relationships with outside groups.

In his research on purposive social change Roland Warren (1965) has suggested that three basic types of social change strategies are available. They are:

Collaborative Strategies

Collaborative strategies are appropriate when there is agreement on the issues among affected parties. The primary role of the change agent is that of enabler or catalyst, and his main concern is ensuring that decision-makers have all the necessary information. Even though the successful use of this strategy is limited to those issues on which there is agreement, there is a tendency to attempt to apply this model to a larger range of issues, including those that are disputed. Such attempts are likely to increase the level and intensity of disagreement and conflict. Warren suggests that welfare councils have historically tended to operate in this model.

Campaign Strategies

Campaign strategies are appropriate to situations in which there are issue differences or disputes about whether or not an issue exists or how an issue should be resolved. The primary role of the change agent is that of persuader, and his task is to create a higher salience of the values and interests people have regarding a particular problem, for example, through the use of "educational" campaigns. He may also try to bring pressures to bear on significant persons to make them realize that certain decisions on this problem are in their best interests.

Contest strategies

Contest strategies are appropriate to situations in which there is issue dissensus, a basic disagreement regarding the issues and values involved; the primary role of the change agent is that of contestant in which he competes for power and resources that will affect the direction of decisions about a given problem or issue.

Warren further suggests that contest strategies might be seen as consisting of four types: *(a)* behavior within accepted social norms, for example, legislative debates; *(b)* processes aimed at changing the distribution of power in a community, for example, voter registration and/or political campaigns aimed at unseating certain incumbents; *(c)* behavior that violates community norms, for example, social action or protest activities, such as sit-ins, rent strikes, etc.; *(d)* behavior that might be termed conflict in the stricter sense of the word, for example, harassment of public officials or physical violence.

In a practical sense a number of change strategies are available to the practitioner. Within the framework of the many factors that affect the design of the social change process, the following represent only a sampling of available models:

1. Ombudsman (The American Assembly, 1967).

2. Strategies of coordination (Demone and Newman, 1970; Torrens, 1969).

3. Strategies of community organization (Rothman, 1964; Murphy, 1960).

4. Strategies of community development (Sanders, 1958; Dunham, 1960).

5. Forums, conferences, and seminars (Carter, 1967, pp. 489-498).

6. Bargaining (Brager and Jorrin, 1969).
7. Consensus (Scheff, in press).
8. Consultation (Caplan, 1964; Downs, 1965; Sussman, 1966).
9. Legal strategies (Curran, 1965).
10. Contest (Alinsky, 1945).
11. Self-study and evaluation (Mann, 1957).

ADVOCACY, CONTEST, CONFLICT, AND MILITANCY

Historically, human services organizations have tended to be seen as agents of intervention that stabilized social systems. The settlement house or the mental health clinic, for example, provided a means of stabilizing relationships between persons and their social environment. The concern within these kinds of organizations was that of facilitating an adjustment between a person and his milieu. The cumulative effect of these efforts has generally been to stabilize, not transform, social systems.

Which is probably less true today than earlier in recent history, although the number of human services organizations as agents of system-transformation is still relatively few. However, human services organizations are increasingly becoming involved in advocacy, contest, and conflict; sometimes their style is one of militancy. While it would be inappropriate to end this section without examining some of the problems generated by this change in organizational postures, it is difficult to do more than briefly focus on some of the risks, liabilities and assets, and complexities of these organizational behaviors.

Advocacy might be viewed as assuming a number of forms, with these varying along a continuum of means. A human services organization, or certain of its staff members, might assume the role of advocacy planner, as Peattie (1968) has described it; the role of advocacy litigant, along the lines of Nader's Raiders; the role of advocate militant, such as in the civil rights or rent strikes movements; or the role of violent advocate, such as that referred to by Hofstadter (1970). Or contrariwise, the organization may use moral suasion. Admittedly, these are oversimplified roles or types, but their purpose is to define possible points on a continuum of low to high degrees of intensity or extremism in acting out an advocacy position.

When the intensity of this role increases, it should be noted that a number of other differential properties of the social change process are generated. For example, the extent to which the advocate will be able to exert control over outcomes will be reduced as his role intensity increases. Similarly, the degree of risk to both the advocate, or the advocacy organization, and the group for whom advocacy is being enacted is substantially increased. As intensity of advocacy increases, they may all find themselves and their causes, however worthwhile, in serious jeopardy.

These relationships are hypothetically reflected in Figures 1 and 2:

Whether or not a human service organization should or should not be engaged in an advocacy position is a major issue in itself. Obviously, it will be decided differently under different environmental conditions and constellations and political power. Our feeling is that the role is both a legitimate and viable one, but one that brings with it certain risks and by definition excludes other means of social change. Consequently, an organization should be fully aware of what it is doing and not assume an advocacy posture inadvertently or because of political pressures or support that might vanish under the stress of conflict. After all, organizations are made up of people. They will not work harmoniously with organizations that are attacking them.

It is unfortunate but accurate to say in many instances that if a human services organization does not assume an advocacy position for its client population, no one will. And organizations that have adopted this position

high   high

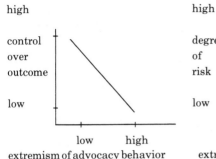

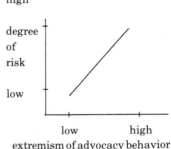

Fig.   1.   The   relationship
between   extremism   of   advocacy behavior and control over
outcome.

Fig.   2.   The   relationship
between   extremism   of   advocacy behavior and the degree
of risk to advocates and constituents.

have been a distinct minority. By and large they have deserved the hostility and charges of irrelevance that have
been aimed at them.

It is also unfortunate but accurate to say that in assuming an advocacy position, a human services organization
is likely to be seen, and perhaps to become, as Peattie
(1968)   described   it,   dangerously   similar   to   other
manipulators of the poor's interests. Further, it is easier
to attack one's friends. They may be more understanding
of political constituencies. Perlman and Jones (1967),
who studied 20 neighborhood service centers, report that
"social action has shown a disconcerting tendency to direct its strongest fire at the allies and benevolent neu-
trals, close at hand, rather than at the more distant enemy." And this makes sense, for according to one Spanish-
speaking American leader, your friends will understand
why it is necessary to sit in on them rather than those
who   are   hostile   or   who   lack   understanding   of   the
genuineness of their cause.

The poor need advocates, and human services organizations can become advocates. But if they do, as we feel
they should, it should be through reason and reality, not
rhetoric.

7. PLANNING CONSTRAINTS

Because planning customarily implies individual or organizational change, it is not surprising that resistance often develops. Influence, power, politics, accommodation, and compromise are key intervening variables. Since it is unlikely that American planners will ever be given sufficient power to guarantee implementation of their recommendations, some accommodation is therefore likely. In fact, the American marketplace mechanism not only assures contest but permits the design of alternative countervailing planning organizations. Recently, this has been identified as advocacy planning, but even without a specific identification it has historically been a part of the American scene.

Often at issue in the politics of planning and change is organizational autonomy and possibly even survival. Simon, Smithburg, and Thompson (1961, p. 453) remind us that the "existing pattern of organizational behavior has qualities of persistence; it is valuable in some way or it would not be maintained."

The following dimensions represent commonly encountered constraints in human services planning:

HOSTILITY

In their analysis of alcoholism planning Demone and Newman (1970) described a series of obstacles. Most important was the hostility toward alcoholics among the various human services professionals. Such a negative set is not directed exclusively to alcoholics, for many groups, including the delinquent, the drug dependent, the criminal, and even the chronically ill and the aged, may face similar attitudes at the hands of the so-called care givers. Other obstacles noted ranged from apathy to personality variations among key actors.

GOALS

The more general, theoretical, and abstract the goals, the more likely it is that agreement can be achieved. It is the selection of subgoals or operating goals and means to be used in achieving them that stimulates controversy. Intraorganizationally, it may require reallocation of resources and roles, while interorganizationally it may imply impingement on the territory of another organization.

Banfield (1962, p. 78), in his analysis of governmental agencies, suggests that the formulation of ends be left vague. "Serious reflection on the ends of the organization, and especially any attempt to state ends in precise and realistic terms, is likely to be destructive of that organization." He believes that the obvious confusion, overlapping, and inconsistency found in public organizations is not accidental but a reflection of the role of public organizations in a democratic society. Required to accommodate to conflicting interests, consistency is seldom possible.

ALTERNATIVES

The ideal-type planning model promotes the identification of alternatives. To what extent do we really have a range of feasible alternatives? The existentialists note the frequency of situations in which man is faced with impossible choices. There is often no clear option between good and evil, no way of avoiding some unpleasantness. Can planners committed to implementation realistically conceptualize the total range of alternatives? In developing state plans for mental health in the early 1960s, the administrators and planners were working within severe boundaries. The states were spending over 90% of their funds in institutions, and the community mental health model, although only one of many options, had already been enacted by Congress, reinforced by NIMH guidelines, and supported by precedents in many states.

When feasibility is included as a criterion, alternatives must always be examined within a context. What do the laws say? What are the system maintenance requirements? What kind of consensus can be identified? What are the chances of success? (Demone, 1965)

SPECIALIZATION AND PROFESSIONS

A major obstacle to social change is specialization. The increasing categorization, proliferation, and specialization of the human services network has produced people whose perspective stems from their professions and categorical areas. In turn these specialists relate to special interest groups. Peer-oriented prestige values dominate. As they rethink their domains and boundaries and especially as they aim for comprehensiveness and relevancy, they find themselves in conflict with other specialists. Psychiatrists are surprised to learn that pediatricians, psychologists, special educators, and vocational rehabilitation counselors also lay claim to competence in retardation. One can predict that such domain and territorial confrontations will become increasingly common, especially as the movement toward human needs and services expands. The "whole man" does not fit the arbitrary boundaries established by the various special interest groups (Newman & Demone, 1969).

Advice to the administrators and planners entering this thicket: Keep your guard up, or be prepared for major changes.

INTERORGANIZATIONAL CONSTRAINTS

Given the various levels of government—federal, state, county, city, and town—and the many governmental organizations that do not reflect these five boundaries but regionalize on an interstate or substate basis, when combined with the various possible types of voluntary agencies—federated, corporate, and independent—whose geographic coverage may in turn be unique, it is clear that maximizing interagency cooperation and planning is confronted with complex territorial barriers.

When these impediments are combined with variable agency goals and objectives that also may be conflicting or overlapping, the problem is further compounded.

In addition, domains may be discrepant. Agency objectives are established intraorganizationally and may be different from those created by other agencies. Competition for funds, sanctions, leadership, staff, and clients are all part of the community scene. (Levine, 1966)

METROPOLITAN CONSTRAINTS

Banfield (1965) describes four basic obstacles to comprehensive metropolitan planning that are inherent in all comprehensive planning, although their specifics may differ.

First he reminds us of the rapidity of change, with much of it unanticipated. Second, he notes that a metropolitan area (or a city) has no objectives. Public purposes are not delimited or operationalized. Agreement occurs on such a generalized level that it begs the question that must be answered. The transition to the third obstacle is obvious: With respect to major policy issues, major differences of opinion exist. (Should low-income housing be supplied in the suburbs? Which should be sacrificed, rapid transit or the automobile?) Finally, Banfield claims that even if we were to agree on goals, we do not have the know-how to achieve them. (How do we educate slum children, eliminate poverty, prevent the growth of ghettos, or build a beautiful city?)

PARTICIPATION

As noted earlier, one of the common strategies to enhance the likelihood of implementation of recommendations is to involve the key actors and organizations in the study and planning process. Although this is a useful and important tactic, it has counterproductive effects as well. Mott (1969, p. 749) notes that those who have a vital stake in the outcome "are likely to influence the questions to be considered, how they are to be approached, the alternative solutions to be considered and the causes of action to be selected."

True it is process, and true it is democratic, but the result of participation is almost always a series of watered-down recommendations reflecting the possible more than the desired. Nevertheless, it is incremental movement and usually positive.

CONSUMER PARTICIPATION

We have already suggested some of the advantages and some of the limits in the current emphasis on participation. The involvement of consumers is a special subcase. Consumers are likely to stress accessibility of services. The provider has the responsibility to include issues of quality. The consumer may demand neighborhood-based specialized services that can only be supplied adequately on a regional level. Hochbaum (1969), in discussing health services, suggests that the fundamental differences are ideological. The health professionals are usually concerned with medical-care considerations, the consumer with social, political, and racial aspects of services.

CONSENSUS

Overlapping with the participation model is one that aims for consensus not only among the planning participants but among all affected organizations. Feasible recommendations with a high potential for implementation are significant components of the consensual model. Its problems are three: *(a)* Some problems are irreconcilable where fundamental differences exist; *(b)* it assumes that all interested parties can be identified and involved prior to the decision-making process; and *(c)* if successful in achieving the first two steps, the agreement usually is composed of a variety of trade-offs that might be acceptable to the participating organizations but may bring about little real change.

The primary problem with the consensual model is that it cannot be used effectively with conflicting issues. When values are divergent or when fundamental organizational patterns are threatened, agreement will never be achieved by consensus, only by coercion or substantial exchange.

CONFRONTATION

An old tactic revived in the mid 1960s—confrontation—has become currently popular as an intervention method. It is also laden with pitfalls and constraints. When individuals and organizations are pushed, they tend not only to push back but to resent the threats and accusations that are necessary to the confrontation model. Further, once confrontation is used, it tends to exclude the use of other social planning and change techniques, for example, collaboration, cooperation, coordination, participation, etc. Following sit-ins, bomb scares, threatening telephone calls, and angry accusations in the press, the organization employing these tactics should not be surprised if the attacked agency fails to cooperate not only with respect to the matter in question but in other issues, also. Later losses may significantly offset immediate gains.

THE TECHNICAL REPORT

Another common planning model is the writing of technical reports. An expert or small group of experts is sanctioned by some organization to study a predetermined problem and to recommend solutions; on paper at least, this resembles the rational-man model. Data are gathered and analyzed, goals determined, alternatives selected, and means to achieve the goals may be included.

That such a report may gather dust is obvious, although if written on a politically "hot" subject, it may gather press if properly handled. Information may be influential, given proper circumstances.

The possible failing of such a model is its naïve assumption that the scientist-planners can be objective and neutral. Mott (1969) notes several sources of bias that are often present. Planners seldom choose the subjects to be studied. Furthermore, once the subject is determined, their professional bias may enter into the criteria that govern the evaluation and selection of courses of action. Prevention or treatment may be emphasized. Causes may be perceived as genetic, environmental, social, or economic.

Since planners are seldom self-employed, at some point they must report back to their organization, one that probably employs an executive and may have a board or elected officials to whom the executive in turn reports. They have colleagues and probably a family.

And to repeat, the problem of implementation is not likely to be organizationally assigned its proper political priority.

MONEY

Unlike the social service system, the health industry until recently has been relatively immune to public attack. As long as low-income people received large amounts of public funds—beginning in the 1930s—especially in periods of relative affluence and high employment, the recipients were subject to widespread criticism. Debtors prisons have a long and proud tradition among Anglo-Saxons, and people can still be imprisoned for nonpayment of debt in some jurisdictions.

As the nation's second largest industry, and as the government picks up one-third of the health bill, the immunity of the health industry from large-scale public criticism is rapidly dissolving. Medicare and Medicaid have heightened public attention. Hospital bills of well over

$100 a day and an industry whose costs are inflating without concommitant increases in either quantity or quality of services are particularly vulnerable to criticism. With health no longer considered a privilege but a right, the public now demands the right to establish policy and insists on accountability.

Wealth and popularity often bring problems, as the health industry is now learning.

8. THE ADMINISTRATIVE PROCESS

Central to the functioning of every organization is the administrative process. No organization can afford to be without both administrative talent, ideas, and technologies, for their absence places an organization's resources in jeopardy and minimizes the effective and creative use of those resources (MacKenzie, 1969). Unfortunately, the full and productive use of administrative talent, ideas, and technologies seems to be the exception rather than the rule in the human service organization.

Cynics have suggested that the "Peter Principle" (Peter and Hull, 1969) has found its most effective application in those organizations that comprise the human services. Historically, many of these organizations have tended to award highest prestige to their most effective practitioners, that is, those professionals who are most competent in their discipline. However, administrative positions have often been assigned to those professionals who are less interested or less able to become highly skilled practitioners. This custom is particularly evident in medicine. Consequently, there has been a tendency for persons who are professionally less competent and subsequently less valued by their peers to rise to the upper strata of human service organizations. Or if they meet all criteria, they are faced with nearly insurmountable negative stereotypes. What is needed is full status and sanctioning for human service professionals and nonprofessionals who have administrative talent and who might choose to carve out administrative careers for themselves. It will occur only when we realize that effective administration requires different skills from effective practice, but ones that are equally complex.

The material in this chapter is designed to shed some light on administrative functions, roles, strategies, and technologies. Although it by no means encompasses all of the highly complex organizational behavior in which administrators engage, hopefully it will give some structure to a neglected, often denigrated, but vitally important element of the human service organization.

ADMINISTRATIVE FUNCTIONS

The functions of persons in administrative or managerial positions have been the subject of numerous writers and researchers. A representative sampling of this work over the past 50 years might include that by such persons as Taylor (1923), Barnard (1938), Roethlisberger (1941), and Likert (1961, 1967), as well as others too numerous to mention in this short space. Summarizing and attempting to extract those factors that seem common to the many and varied approaches to the study and practice of administration and, further, attempting to view these factors in terms of human services organizations, the following would seem to be important and consensually validated administrative functions:

Data Input Monitoring

What are the sources of data that the organization uses in examining its performance? How are the data used? How reliable and how valid are these data? Effective administration requires that the monitoring of organizational data input be performed in such a way as to prevent the organization from developing faulty bases for its internal decision-making, hence risking its resources through erroneous problem-solving strategies stemming from these decisions.

Problem Conceptualizing

Although no one administrator can be expected to be

the problem conceptualizer for his organization, it is incumbent upon him to ensure that this function is being performed in the organization. An effective division of labor and a matching of the skills and interests of individual employees with their actual organizational assignments are strategies that are likely to make it easier to carry out this function.

Unfortunately, dysfunctional organizational and/or professional norms in human service organizations, anachronistic merit systems, or personal insecurities and inadequacies often lead to a funneling of problem conceptualizing into limited administrative offices and channels.

Problem Analysis

What are the relevant variables both within a problem and surrounding that problem that need to be brought to bear on effective problem analysis? The issue here, as in problem conceptualizing, is to stimulate the appropriate persons and establish the necessary conditions. The more open the communication channels, the more likely there will be multiple information input leading to a relatively accurate consensual validation of problem analysis.

Organizational Decisions and Action

Where and how are decisions made in organizations? What mechanisms are there to generate action on those decisions? Some recent research (Harshbarger, 1971) has indicated that small groups are far more accurate in solving problems if they make decisions through consensus rather than through an autocratic decision-making process, even though, under both conditions, there was a free and open transmission of communication. Further, and most importantly, the research suggested that persons would be likely, if given the choice, to choose a centralized or relatively autocratic, rather than a consensual, decision-making structure. Thus, what we might desire in the way of decision-making structures and what is most likely to be the most accurate kind of decision-making structure may often be contradictory.

Going beyond how decisions are made, an effective administrator must deal with the problems of generating feasible outcomes and actions to implement these decisions. Given the emphasis that human services organizations place on group and organizational process, there is a tendency to substitute process for outcome in organizational decision-making. That is, human services professionals are so accustomed to "feeling good" during and after meaningful group experiences that they tend to transfer a point of view that is appropriate to the therapeutic process to the organizational decision-making process.

Effective organizational decision-making and implementation have never been the long suits of human services organizations. A much more critical examination of these organizational functions has been long needed.

Purposive Follow-Through

Effective involvement, decisions, and action are not enough. There must be the kind of follow-through that ensures that the job will be done or further decisions rendered to add the necessary resources to complete the task. Clarification of the task, a work program, and a time schedule are all useful management tasks. Otherwise, the best laid plans . . .

Feedback

Every organization must operate with multilevel feedback designed to alter or sustain decisions throughout the organization. Unfortunately, human services organizations, with their professional biases and ideologies permeating the everyday work process, have tended to substitute professionally appropriate value judgments for relatively hard data on outcomes of decisions. Although we give lip service to relatively scientific and empirical bases of feedback, the kinds of information to which we are responsive and the kinds of information that we are likely to manufacture and transmit are replete with our professional ideologies that, by definition, are slanted and one-sided.

Beyond this problem there are the problems of what, among relatively hard data, shall constitute feedback and what information-transmitting structures will lead to reliable information transmission. Outcome rather than process information needs sanctioning. Moreover, will the information be received and assimilated by persons who need to know? And finally managers need to be trained to integrate data into decision-making.

Generating Organizational Change

No environment is static, although we sometimes seem to act as if this were the case. An effective administrator must both monitor changes in the external and internal environments of the organization as well as think through the realistic possibilities and strategies for change in the organization. As Bennis et al. (1969) have indicated, this is by no means a simple problem, rather one that demands that the agent of change have a credible, workable plan for organizational change as well as a fairly accurate view of the consequences of those changes.

Human Relations and Communication

Intimately tied to the many other functions that have been mentioned, the problems of human relations and communication that arise in a human services organization are myriad and infinitely complex. They demand, to a greater or lesser degree, virtually constant monitoring of group and interpersonal processes in the organization. Given the very human focus of the activities of most human services organizations, one might expect there to be an abundance of resident experts in these problems. Unfortunately, the pressures and problems of the human services organization often have the same divisive and communication-inhibiting effects that one finds in many other kinds of organizations. It is incumbent upon the administrator to keep the social machinery oiled and functioning. (For a humorous and perceptive account of this process, the reader might read parts of Jim Bouton's *Ball Four* in which he describes social interventions by the manager of the Seattle Pilot baseball team, interventions designed to ease tension and open up communication among often hostile teammates.)

ADMINISTRATIVE STRATEGIES AND TECHNOLOGIES

Democratic Management

One of the most currently popular sociotechnical means of reaching decisions, democratic management, as described by Bennis (1965), injects a note of pluralism into organizational decision-making practices that have too often been relatively autocratic. As Gomberg (1966) has noted in a critical commentary, this management strategy has become one of the more modish, avant-garde philosophies of students and leading academic figures in prestigious business schools, as well as in many complex organizations.

Slater and Bennis (1964) describe democratic management as containing maximum communication independent of organizational status; consensual decision-making; organizational influence of the individual based on knowledge and competence; an organizational atmosphere permitting free expression and open communication networks; and a focus on human needs and concerns, one that accepts the inevitability of confrontation between the individual and the organization.

The issues involved in the uses of democratic management strategies in reaching organizational decisions are multiple. Gomberg (1966) suggests that it may be more of a value framework than a management strategy; that is, it may be a guiding philosophy but practical only under certain, as yet unknown, specifiable conditions. Bennis (1970), in a later view of the strategy, reaches similar conclusions. When Bennis the scholar turns to Bennis the actor, even more complexities are noted. (See his article, "Searching for the 'Perfect' University President," in the April 1971 *Atlantic*.) As an academic vice-president and a candidate for a college presidency, he presents a witty and penetrating analysis of leadership in complex organizations. At the core of the problem is where, when, and under what conditions these management practices are likely to lead to more effective organizational adaptation. Can this model, which was originally designed as a function of the experiences of certain large, task-force-centered consulting firms, be appropriately extended to the human services?

In addition, it might be helpful to consider the model as twofold, one that is aimed at both the communication processes and networks in organizations, as well as with the specific decision-making practices of that organization. In terms of the former, the model would seem to hold promise for human service organizations, that is, greater openness of communication networks across intra- and interorganizational boundaries would seem desirable. In terms of the latter, and specifically the uses of consensual decision-making, the model as yet lacks enough application to specify its potential for long-range versus short-range decisions, consumer versus professional decisions, community versus intraorganizational decisions, and a host of other yet untested dimensions.

Critical Path Method

Among the newer technologies for reaching organizational decisions is the critical path method. Basically, it refers to a set of activities, following an adequate and consensually validated definition of the current problem, to determine the necessary activities to move toward problem solution, the sequence of those activities and the requirements in terms of activity time and other organizational resources.

Originating in engineering, the critical path method forces a relatively graphic description of the job to be done, the time necessary to accomplish it, and the sequence of events. In addition, it facilitates a relatively accurate estimate of the organizational costs involved, leading to further budgetary and personnel planning.

BUDGET AND FINANCE

Planning, programming, budgeting systems (PPBS), a concept that swept the federal government during the late 1960s, is currently being adopted by organizations throughout the human services. Early forerunners of PPBS date back prior to World War I; early applications were tried in the Department of Agriculture and the Tennessee Valley Authority. The Hoover Commission Report of 1949 highlighted the performance budget (Taubenhaus, Hamlin, & Wood, 1957). Put simply, general organizational objectives are validated, and organizational activities that contribute toward the achievement of these objectives are identified, separated, and classified. Costs are then identified, and a functional program budget is developed that specifies the relative costs of each program and its components. Following these activities, it is then possible to make some decisions regarding the attained benefits, in terms of improvement, say, of service delivery systems, when these benefits are contrasted with their respective costs. In short, it is a means of arriving at estimates of cost-effectiveness, or cost-benefits ratios.

The evolutionary components and processes involved in the development of PPBS have included such technologies as performance budgets, program budgets, functional budgets, and cost-benefit analysis. In less than two decades accountants and systems analysts have provided the human services with increasingly complex and sophisticated procedures for examining their activities, but the adoption of these technologies has been slow, problematic, and hesitant.

Two problems are paramount in the uses of PPBS. One is the process of social change that leads to the adoption of PPBS as a sociotechnical system. How can this come about? What is necessary in related organizational changes (e.g., the existing decision-making structures) to implement effectively such a technology? What are the organizational change problems, strategies, programs, and outcomes that must be taken into account? What will be required in the way of talented change agents?

The other problem has to do with PPBS itself. Not only do human service organizations often lack the relatively "hard" data that other kinds of organizations might have; there is contained in the suggestion that PPBS is a better decision-making system the implicit notion that its use will permit accurate, effective decisions. Unfortunately, nothing could be farther from the truth. In the human services ultimate decisions regarding the uses of organizational resources are based on relative, not absolute, differences and on moral-laden value judgments. Is it "better" to rehabilitate a client with an appendectomy, an AFDC mother, an adult male alcoholic, an amputee, or a youthful drug-dependent person? (And what about programs for the aged or chronically ill?) What criteria are to be used? Who asks the questions? Whose opinion is to be final? Can accurate cost figures be established? What is the basis for the prognosis? The translation into quantitative data may be illusory. As difficult as client-oriented objectives may be, they are relatively simple compared to efforts at objectifying prevention or efforts to change systems, subsystems, and organizations.

PERSONNEL PRACTICES

In human service organizations it has been the public agencies that have led the way in designing merit systems and organizing fringe benefits. Developed not as a positive step forward but as a means to control the spoils system, they have created problems of their own, particularly in rigid job descriptions and classifications. However, in recent years in the federal government, many states and some large and middle-sized cities, have attempted to move from various forms of negative controls to progressive personnel management systems.

As with most management functions personnel administration has become a function of both personnel specialists and line officials in operating agencies, with its basic objective, as Stahl (1962) has noted, that of maintaining effective human resources and human relations in the organization. It is one of the fundamental procedures necessary to get a job done. As a specialized function, it is concerned with such problems as developing and carrying out employee relations policy, handling problems as they arise, working with organized labor, developing methods of recruiting new employees and of evaluating employee performance, organizing and maintaining communication links between employees and management, and maximizing employee potential and maintaining personnel policies.

As specialized departments in large organizations few personnel departments fulfill all these functions equally well, even though the professionalization of the personnel field has lifted its sights and standards. In smaller organizations not justifying separate specialized staff, such roles are usually enacted by one of the professional staff and the office manager. In fact, such assignments are strongly advisable, for adequate procedures are more likely to be developed if a clear role assignment is made.

Stahl (1962) describes the following broad duties as typical of personnel practices: (a) developing policies and instructions; (b) job analysis and evaluation (in collaboration with supervisors); *(c)* recruiting, interviewing, processing, and evaluating; *(d)* salary and wage administration; *(e)* advising on employee relations; *(f)* developing and assisting in performance standards and evaluation; *(g)* staff training and development; *(h)* advising and participating in staff separation from service; *(i)* informing employees of their rights and obligations; *(j)* maintaining employee records; *(k)* personnel research; *(l)* and public relations (of nonspecialized nature).

Widely recommended as a critical management ingredient is a formal employee performance appraisal mechanism that is carefully linked to salary increments. Unfortunately, in the human services these evaluation and feedback systems have often become dysfunctional through the interference of professional ideologies that have contaminated decisions regarding what behaviors are relevant and appropriate to the positions and roles being evaluated.

Ideally, the goals of such a system are: *(a)* to motivate employees; *(b)* to discriminate between employees with high and low potential; *(c)* to improve management's capacity to make decisions about salary increases, promotions, and transfers; *(d)* to develop an objective rating system for use by supervisors; and *(e)* to inform employees how they are viewed by the organization in order to estimate future opportunities.

The basic models are two: *(a)* a system in which employees are rated against each other and *(b)* one in which the individual's performance is measured against preestablished objectives and/or contrasted with his own previous experience.

Thompson and Dalton (1970) suggest that an objective-focused approach may be a functional alternative that: *(a)* permits improved capacity by one employee without automatically requiring that another employee receive a lower rating; *(b)* does not require the manager to play "God"; *(c)* reduces the focus on personality traits; *(d)* is future oriented, anticipating rewards that motivate; *(e)* allows most or even all employees in an organiza-

tion to feel a sense of accomplishment and movement if
this is deserved; *(f)* is flexible for both the supervisor and
the employee; *(g)* and permits open rather than closed
systems accommodating variations in the increasing
number of complex multiorganizations.

Ford (1969, p. 35), writing from the perspective of the
Bell System, came to a similar conclusion. He noted that
job turnover increased despite better two-way communication, improved salary and benefit plans, supervision, industrial relations, and management policies. In
addition, better employees left at a faster rate than less
valued employees.

In conclusion, it is not that money, benefits, human
relations, and organizations are unimportant, but most
important is the job itself. Is it meaningful? Is it responsible? Is it stimulating? Ford recommends that we focus
on improving the nature of the job. Too often we have
treated a job as though "a job is a job is a job." He concludes (1969, p. 35): "Use me well. Let my life mean something."

ADMINISTRATIVE ROLE PROPERTIES

Various writers have pointed to the many role properties of effective administrators, for example, the administrator as actor (Batten, in Sonthoff, 1964); as organizational catalyst (Hower and Orth, in Sonthoff); as
guardian of organizational resources (Ewing, in
Sonthoff); as friend and counselor (Moment and Zalez-
nik, in Sonthoff); and as a technician in human relationships (Sayles, in Sonthoff). It is possible that such a list
could be extended *ad infinitum.*

With so many alternative and legitimate roles, it is
clear that the first consideration must be the capacity to
be able to shift roles comfortably, frequently, accurately,
and effectively. In the complex and kaleidoscopic demands of human service organizations, perhaps the
most definable characteristic of the administrative role
is not what it is but that it is constantly in flux. An ina-

bility to perform this behavioral shift with comfort will take its psychological and physiological toll in the human outcomes created by high levels of stress. The result is too often seen in both lowered tenure of position occupancy and in the lowered reliability of performance of role incumbents.

CONCLUSION

In his provocative book *Up the Organization* (1970), Robert Townsend reminds us to take both our technologies and our organizations with a grain of salt. Very often, Townsend suggests, the success of complex organizations is not because of the way they operate but in spite of it.

9. THE FUTURE

A DEFINITION OF FUTURISM

Eldredge (1968, p. 382) offers a preliminary operational definition of futurism:

> ... first, the long-range projection of sociocultural change; second, the search for independent and semi-independent variables responsible for this change; and, third, the attempt to manipulate these variables toward long-range goals in a feedback planning process.

By the application of scientific or disciplined means it is presumed that society can make better use of its limited resources. It can serve to identify potential future trouble spots. It can help to extend future options (Eldredge, 1968).

Traditionally, futurists have focused on economic concerns, although recently the interests of physical and social planners have extended its functions to larger socio-political-demographic-ecologic-economic-ethical issues.

Myrdal (1968) in his analysis of Asian poverty illustrates the interrelation of ethical issues. What is required to reduce poverty, according to Myrdal, is a new set of political-economic values, for no government can effectively operate in contradistinction to societal norms that sanction sloth, laziness, superstitution, mismanagement, and corruption.

Structural changes will be impotent against such overwhelming counterproductive standards.

WHY FUTURE PLANNING?

Although there is no qualitative measure of social change, the number of patents taken out annually at the U.S. Census Office may give some indication of a change rate. Since 1850 it can be roughly plotted as an exponential curve, one that is highly accelerative. Clearly, cumulative technology is exponential, for if inventions are new combinations of existing elements, then the broader the base the easier it is to invent.

Presumably, social inventions are similarly knowledge based and, certainly, social change is strongly related to changes in technology. Alvin Toffler (1970, p. 89) in writing on "future shock," posits a picture of geometric change:

> Milleniums of change will be compressed into the next 30 or 40 years, as a wholly novel civilization—superindustrialism—explodes into being in our midst. "This new society will embody values radically different from today's with the drive for material success subordinated to bizarre new aesthetic, religious, moral and social goals. It will be crammed with new forms of antibureaucratic organization—rapidly shifting, kinetic, ad-hocracies. It will offer a dazzling variety of choice with respect to products, culture, jobs and life styles. Yet the single most important feature of this new society will be its pace.

Donald N. Michael (1967, p. 888) generally concurs, concluding that the results will ". . . alter the very core of our way of life, values, beliefs, and aspirations over a 50-year perspective." His may be a conservative estimate.

More specific is Platt (1969, p. 115) who describes the rate of change as an "S curve."

> In the last century, we have increased our speed of communication by a factor of 10^7; our speed of travel by 10^2; our speeds of data handling by 10^6; our energy resources by 10^3; our power of weapons by 10^6; our ability to control diseases by something like 10^2; and our rate of population growth to 10^3 times what it was a few thousand years ago.

Extrapolation would lead one to expect even greater changes in the future.

Nuclear war, famine, poverty, overpopulation, and pollution are but a few of the immediate major threats to our survival. Thus the capacity of our formal organizations to respond to crisis and to change becomes even more vital. In New York City in 1968 school racial conflict and teacher, garbage, police, and longshoreman's strikes all occurred within a few days of each other. Perhaps our administrative crises share the same "S curve" of technological change. Unfortunately, our organizations are rarely, if ever, prepared to cope with simultaneous multiple crises.

As organizations need stability, so does man. They both need predictability, some sense of control over their own destiny. Anarchy has always been quickly repressed even if retrogression and loss of individual freedom is the result. An assumption of the mental health field is that if man does not learn to cope with the individual crisis as it occurs, anxiety, bewilderment, and irritability are likely to develop. If the crises pile up on each other in an endless exponential cycle, then breakdown and mental illness are possible results. Alternative coping mechanisms—drugs, alcohol, dropping out, and communes—are variously adaptive and maladaptive.

Bell (1967) describes four principal bases of change in our society: *(a)* technological development; *(b)* the diffusion of goods and privileges throughout our society; *(c)* structural changes, particularly the centralization of the political system and the husbanding of human capital, and *(d)* the relation of the United States to the remainder of the world.

Future predictions range along a continuum of a world with justice, dignity, humanity, and autonomy to one that is filled with injustice, overpopulated, polluted, and surviving on a subsistence diet in an all-encompassing state. Automation is seen as a boon to problem-solving as well as a means of depriving us of our privacy and self. Improved management skills are touted both as freeing man from drudgery and as depriving him of the right to democratic participation.

ORGANIZATION AND SYSTEM CHANGES

Ideology and Service Delivery Systems

Fundamental to the changing order of the human service system are the ideological changes going on in American society. They are variously described as changes in the moral order from integrity and wholeness to honesty and antihypocrisy (Dixon, 1968), from absolutism to relativism, and from pragmatism and simplicity to existentialism.

These values, these folkways and mores, find themselves imbedded in public policy not necessarily as a result of any conscious effort but in the way key decisionmakers respond to issues. The attack on scientism and professionalism, if continued, will certainly undermine professionally developed health and welfare programs. Dixon (1968, p. 259) states:

> The feeling is that an orderly establishment creates a premature closure on authority—that it necessarily thwarts the individual. Progress must be antiauthoritarian; responsibility must be exercised in role, not in rule.

Now, the professional is told, local availability of services and community control are more important than quality. Task analysis and differentiation of function permit the development of new paraprofessionals or technicians. But this development conflicts with the increasing hostility toward specialization, for paraprofessionals are by definition limited specialized extensions of their professional surrogates. Quality control, a logical extension of the roles of government and professions, is undermined by expressions of the morality of equality of opportunity and the effort to compensate for centuries of discrimination of selected minority groups.

Health in the 1970s

Hilleboe (1968) has ventured some predictions about

the nature of the American health industry in the 1970s. *(a)* The bulk of expenditures will remain in the acute and surgical illnesses requiring hospitalization; improvement in vaccines, increased transplantation, and an increasing blurring between public preventive and private clinical medicine are also likely. *(b)* The fields of rehabilitation and biomedical engineering offer considerable promise, and the proportion of the health dollar expended in chronic illness is expected to increase steadily. *(c)* In mental illness, addictive disorders, and retardation, increased attention will be paid to social causation and treatment, although slow but steady understanding of biomedical factors will also take place. The program focus will continue to shift from the institution to the community. Mental health and generic care-giving programs will be increasingly linked. *(d)* Increasing attention to maternal and child health, nutrition and family planning, can be expected. More concern with the prenatal period and the first few years of life is likely in response to recent research about the importance of these years. *(e)* Acute communicable diseases are still serious problems in economically depressed urban and rural areas. A massive attack would allow for substantial return on investment. *(f)* Accidental and occupational hazards, injuries, and deaths will continue to grow. Primary prevention by manipulation of the agent and environment is very hopeful.

The public concern with environmental issues, which began in the late 1960s, is likely to level off in the early 1970s, although the problems themselves will continue to increase. The essential issue of the 1970s will be to retain sufficient public interest to force the necessary changes and controls. One major recent step, broadening the base of concern beyond a small cult of conservationalists, promises some modest breakthroughs.

Changing Organizational Models

Dixon (1968, p. 263) suggests that "it may be pure

fantasy to think of today's hospital as having the capacity to be a community health center."

Two principal options seem to be possible. One is to extend the general hospital into the community. The other is to develop community health centers that extend back into the hospital. Lacking a comparable systematic facility base (as general hospitals), the social welfare system has moved toward a multiservice, neighborhood service, or comprehensive service model roughly organized along catchment lines. Despite the continued emphasis on all of these models there is reason to believe that each contains major structural defects and that the 1970s will see a new focus on availability, guarantee of equal access to, and continuity of service via an extended linkage and referral system that may not deliver major services on its own. Such a network model implies an acceptance of the pluralistic nature of our society and attempts to maximize the assets and control the deficits of this system. Another element of the pluralistic model will be alternative models accommodating to various regional idiosyncracies and encouraging flexibility.

Multiorganization Complexes

Thompson (1967, p. 157) states that social purposes in modern societies increasingly exceed the capacities of complex organizations, and call instead for action by multiorganization complexes.

Space exploration, hydroelectric dams, and multistate port authorities are examples of the combining of resources from a variety of sources to achieve a goal beyond the capacity of any given organization. These alliances may be *ad hoc* or may reflect mergers bringing about multiorganizations. What should be clear is that multiorganizations need not be large nor the result of advances in technology and hardware. For an example on the smallest scale, voluntary community-planning councils with multiple functions are multiorganizations. The complexity of the human services field is certain to bring about new, more complex, and probably larger organizations. That this will conflict with the goals of community control is also clear.

Postbureaucracy

Classical structure implies clearly delimited rules and regulations governing goals, functions, and responsibilities in order to maximize efficiency. The chain of command, best exemplified by the military, goes from top to bottom. Unfortunately, this model, effective in many ways, is contrary to many cherished beliefs, such as democracy and participation, among others. Ever-increasing technology and specialization requiring open management responsive to new ideas is in part antithetical to the traditional bureaucratic structure.

These combined forces are gradually transforming the classic arrangement into a more open, modified version. The "maple tree," partially collegial model of organizations permits a freer interchange and communication (up and down), less individual supervision, and a greater team orientation.

Bennis (1969, pp. 44-45) has hypothesized a breakdown of contemporary management (i.e., bureaucracy) for four major reasons:

> (1) rapid and unexpected change; (2) growth in size beyond what is necessary for the work being done (e.g., inflation caused by bureaucratic overhead and tight controls, impersonality caused by sprawls, outmoded rules, and organizational rigidities); (3) complexity of modern technology, in which integration between activities of very diverse, highly specialized competence is required; (4) a change in managerial values toward more humanistic democratic practices.

The new leadership concept, according to Bennis (1969, pp. 51, 61), contains four kinds of competencies:

> (1) Knowledge of large, complex human systems;
> (2) practical theories of intervening and guiding these

systems, theories that encompass methods for seeding,
nurturing, and integrating individuals and groups;
(3) interpersonal competence, particularly the sensi-
tivity to understand the effects of one's own behavior
on others and how one's own personality shapes his particular leadership style and value system;
(4) a set of values and competencies which enables one
to know when to confront and attack if necessary and
when to support and provide the psychological safety so
necessary for growth.

Shick (1970, p. 18) suggests that as we move into the
postindustrial state the role and structure of government
will shift to a focus on "concerting the polity and the
economy to achieve public objectives. As a result, the government changes from a *doer* of public activities to a dis-
tributor of public benefits." The welfare bureaucracy will
be dismantled. Instead of thousands of governmental
units and social worker-bureaucrats investigating recipients and requiring "casework," the system will be centralized and automated. Based on some form of guaran-
teed annual income adjusted to the cost of living, mod-
eled organizationally after the Internal Revenue Service,
including its programmed and sampling monitoring procedures, the indignities of investigation will be severely
limited. A similar move can be seen in discussions about
national health insurance and in education. It requires
an increasing transfer of controls from the legislative to
the executive branches, and while subject to resistance
on the part of the legislative branch, the transfer is
inevitable as the individual forms of control continue to
break down, accompanied by a rapid cost escalation.

The Contract and Grant-in-Aid Mechanism

Another significant change, as implied above, will be
the alteration of the government's direct personal service
role. It will subsidize grant-in-aid and contract direct services, giving the government better management controls and enhancing its capacity to alter priorities. The
increasing blurring of public and private functions and

the further development of quasi-private and quasi-public organizations will continue. A new form of human service marketplace will be the result (Shick, 1970).

In turn, government will need fewer and better trained personnel with professional and technical competence. Establishing guidelines, writing contracts, and monitoring standards, they will be working closely with senior contractee personnel, and as such they will have to be paid comparably.

Cost Control Budgets

Whatever the form, it is clear that budget control mechanisms will be an accepted administrative arrangement in human services organizations. Attempts to objectify budgetary analysis will continue, albeit with enormous difficulty. Combined with sophisticated information systems, management tools are likely to be substantially enhanced.

Industry and Social Welfare

Profit-making in the human services represents a significant future development. As the health industry approaches 10% of the GNP, and the production, distribution, and consumption of knowledge 30% of the GNP, it is clear that health and education will no longer be the principal domain of do-gooders, academicians, or physicians. Such an enormous economic potential is ripe for the "social-industrial complex." Although proprietary hospitals have not gained a substantial foothold in the health industry, nor profit-making institutions in the educational field, in recent years the nursing home, homemaker, and day-care center have recently invited considerable for-profit investment. The Job Corps program similarly excited some brief interest, as did the Peace Corps. The growth of the pharmaceutical industry is well known, and the knowledge industry now contains many of our corporate giants.

The underlying issue rests on control. Who establishes the goals, sets the priorities, and monitors the system? Michael Harrington (1967, pp. 58, 60) suggests:

> What is at stake is nothing less than how the Americans of the twenty-first century are going to think and live. . . . For when business methods are sincerely and honestly applied to urban problems, with very good intentions, they still inevitably lead to anti-social results. It is exactly when cross concerns are not paramount that the real problem—the inapplicability of business methods and priorities to the crisis of the cities—emerges most clearly.

Harrington may be overreacting, but certain trends are clearly evident: The human services complex is a growth industry, and the profit-making sector is moving into this enlarging arena. Substantial changes are ensured—as are the social-developmental risks.

New Technologies for Management

Although most discussion of technology focuses on the physical or hardware side, as noted earlier, there are a number of social or soft-ware developments with equally significant implications. The focus on new result-oriented budgeting systems, operational research, simulation, systems analysis, social and economic planning, the linkage of function to structure, new forms of organizational analysis, games theory, and programmed learning are illustrative of these developments.

Necessary to many of these tools is the modern complex computer that permits the aggregation and analysis of large amounts of data. The major factor limiting its use is the lack of skilled personnel to exploit these developing technologies in relation to the human condition. It is already quite clear that many of our most cherished social institutions and values are under attack and likely will be increasingly so in the next generation. Michael Harrington (1967, p. 890) states:

> Such concepts as private investment, the nation, state, privacy, Federal, state and local prerogatives, free enterprise, freedom of science, these and other terms which carry with them a variety of deep beliefs and needs may be so transformed as to be unrecognizable or disappear altogether.

As a consequence, Michael Harrington (p. 891) predicts the development of regional-size educational systems and the dissolution of local school districts; a conflict between information systems and privacy; and priority setting conflicting with private and business freedom.

FUTURE-ORIENTED CONSTRAINTS

That Soviet Russia has had a future-oriented approach to the solution of major social ills has served to constrain comparable American development. Particularly antithetical to American values were the post-World War II Russian five-year plans that were perceived as mechanisms of social control.

Eldredge (1968) suggests that the major Western effort most resembling macro-future planning was that found in the quasi-democratic Fifth French Republic. It was designed to improve France's economic status by influencing the development of private industry. This regionally focused "indicative planning" demonstrated a future-oriented capability not found elsewhere in the Western world. Its sector-oriented industrial base may account for its general acceptance.

CONCLUSION

The service maze is living up to its psychological analogy. As it becomes increasingly difficult to negotiate, specialists become increasingly remote, and depersonalization accelerates, more money is expended, and both service gaps and overlap are more obvious; we have both a present and future problem.

Equally important, increasing population, urbanization, congestion, mobility, sharpening of class and social differences, and continued ethnic tensions are helping to create a feeling of alienation from the decision-making and increasingly technically oriented care-giving systems (Newman & Demone, 1969).

The increasing interest in modern management and planning technologies suggested earlier in this monograph reflect some current answers to the need to humanize, rationalize, and economize. It is clear the task will not be an easy one and will probably become exponentially more difficult as each year passes without a major solution.

Newman and Demone (1969) recommended four steps that, taken together, would be of some help: (a) The full exploitation of technology; (b) the development of strong, competent government; (c) citizen participation at the policy level; and (d) program management procedures that focus on the consumer not the provider.

As noted earlier, we have substantially increased our ability to manage large numbers of variables via the computer. Data analysis, simulation, and fiscal management are all enhanced.

But this escalation of technology is correlated with further estrangement between the technocrat and the citizen, and complex organizations and their consumers. The separation of policy-making from implementation and the design of methods to involve the citizen in the major decisions are critical issues.

But authority cannot be shared if it does not exist, and executives cannot open up their organizations if their activities are stifled with detail and their authority unclear and ambiguous. Agencies and institutions cannot share that which they do not possess. McGeorge Bundy (1968) suggests that the executive branch of government must be strengthened if it is to fulfill effectively its responsibilities. Lacking clearly concentrated authority and responsibility, constrained by laws laden with detail and restricting flexibility, hampered by tables of or-

ganization that make subordinates essentially independent, the governmental executive must be strengthened
if government is to work.

People and their problems are not categorical despite
their proliferated organizations.

REFERENCES

Alinsky, S. *Reveille for radicals*. Chicago: University of Chicago
Press, 1945.

Ardell, D. B. Urban-planning/health-planning relationships.
American Journal of Public Health, 1969, **59**, 2051-2055.

Aronson, J. B. Planning for community health services. *Public
Health Reports,* 1964, **79**, 1101-1106.

Baker, F. General systems theory research, and medical care. In A.
Sheldon, F. Baker, & C. McLaughlin (Eds.), *Systems and medical care.*
Cambridge, Mass.: MIT Press, 1970.

Baker, F., & Schulberg, H. C. Community health caregiving systems:
Integration of interorganizational networks. In A. Sheldon, F. Baker, &
C. McLaughlin (Eds.), *Systems and medical care.* Cambridge, Mass.:
MIT Press, 1970.

Banfield, E. C. Ends and means in planning. In Maileck, S., & Van
Ness, E. H. (Eds.), *Concepts and issues in administrative behavior.*
Englewood Cliffs, N.J.: Prentice-Hall, 1962.

Banfield, E. C. The uses and limitations of metropolitan planning in
Massachusetts. In *Issues and problems of Boston metropolitan area development.* Boston, Mass.: Metropolitan area planning council, 1965.

Barnard, C. *The functions of the executive.* Cambridge; Harvard University Press, 1938.

Beck, B. M. Community control: A distraction, not an answer. *Social
Work,* 1969, **14**, (4), 14-20.

Bell, D. The year 2000—Trajectory of an idea. *Daedalus: Proceedings
of the American Academy of Arts and Sciences,* 1967, **96**, 639-651.

Bennis, W. Beyond bureaucracy. *Trans-Action,* 1965, **2**, 31-35.

Bennis, W. G. & Slater, P. E. *The temporary society.* New York:
Harper, 1968.

Bennis, W. G., & Harris, T. G. Organic populism. *Psychology Today,*
February, 1970. 3 (9), 48-54, 68-70.

Bennis, W. G., Benne, K. D., & Chin, R. (Eds.) *The planning of
change.* New York: Holt, Rinehart, 1969.

Bennis, W. G. Post-bureaucratic leadership. *Trans-Action,* 1969, **6** (9),
44-61.

Bennis, W. A funny thing happened on the way to the future. *American Psychologist,* 1970, **25**, 595-608.

Biddle, F. J., & Thomas, E. J. *Role theory: concepts and research.*
New York: Wiley, 1966.

Blake, R. R., & Mouton, J. S. *The managerial grid.* Houston: Gulf Pub-
lishing Co., 1961.

Blau, P. M. *Bureaucracy in modern society.* New York: Random House, 1956.

Brager, G. A., and Jorrin, V. Bargaining: A method in community change. *Social Work,* 1969, **14,** (4), 73-83.

Braybrooke, D., & Lindbloom, C. *A strategy of decision.* New York: Free Press, 1963.

Bulletin of the Foundation Library Center, 1968, **9** (3), 55-56.

Bundy, M. Godkin Lectures, Harvard University, 1968.

Caplan, G. *Principles of preventive Psychiatry.* New York: Basic Books, 1964.

Carter, L. F. The traveling seminar and conference for the implementation of educational innovation. In *Social Research in Federal Domestic Programs.* Committee on Government Operations, House of Representatives. Washington, D.C.: U.S. Government Printing Office, 1967.

Committee on Environment of the American Public Health Association. Environmental factors in health planning. *American Journal of Public Health,* 1963, **50,** 358-360.

Curran, W. J. Progress in mental health legislation. Address given at Seventeenth Annual Mental Hospital Institute, San Francisco, September 1965.

Daniels, A. H. The captive professional: Bureaucratic limitations in the practice of military psychiatry. *Journal of Health and Social Behavior,* 1969, **10,** 255-265.

Demone, H. W., Jr. The Limits of rationality in planning. *Community Mental Health Journal,* 1965, **1,** 375-381.

Demone, H. W., Jr., Spivack, M., & McGrath, M. Decision-making issues in the development of community mental health centers. Paper presented at the New England Psychological Association, Boston, November 1966.

Demone, H. W., Jr., & Newman, E. Mental health planning and coordination: Can it really be accomplished? In H. Gruenbaum (Ed.), *The Practice of Community Mental Health:* Boston: Little, Brown, 1970.

Demone, H. W., Jr. Human services at state and local levels and the integration of mental health. In G. Caplan (Ed.), *American handbook of psychiatry.* Vol. 2, New York: Basic Books, 1973.

Dixon, J. D. The health agenda for the future. *Milbank Memorial Fund Quarterly,* 1968, **46,** (259-264,Pt. 2).

Downs, A. Some thoughts on giving people economic advice. *The American Behavioral Scientist,* 1965.

Dunham, A. Community development. *Social Work Yearbook,* 1960, **14,** 178-186.

Eldredge, H. W. Futurism in planning for developing countries. *American Institute of Planners Journal,* 1968, **34,** 382-384.

Emery, F. E., & Trist, E. L. The causal texture of organizational environments. *Human Relations,* 1965, **18,** 1-10, 21-32.

Evan, W. M. The organizational set: Toward a theory of interorganizational relationships. In J. D. Thompson (Ed.), *Approaches to organizational design.* Pittsburgh: University of Pittsburgh Press, 1966.

Feingold, E. The changing political character of health planning. *American Journal of Public Health,* 1969, **59,** No. 5, 803-808.

Fogelson, F., and Demone, H. W., Jr. Program change through mental health planning. *Community Mental Health Journal,* 1969, **5,** 3-13.

Ford, R. M. The obstinate employee. *Psychology Today,* 1969, **3** (6), 32-35.

Freed, H. M., & Miller, L. Planning a community mental health program: A case history. *Community Mental Health Journal,* 1971, in press.

Freed, H. M., Schroder, D., & Baker, B. The west side story. Unpublished manuscript, Illinois State Psychiatric Institute, 1970.

Friedmann, J. Notes on societal action. *American Institute of Planners Journal,* 1969. **35,** 311-318.

Gardner, J. W. How to prevent organizational dry rot. *Harper's,* 1965, **231** (1385), 20-26.

Gilbert, N. Maximum feasible participation? A Pittsburgh encounter. *Social Work,* 1969, **14,** (3), 84-92.

Gilmore, J. S., Ryan, J. D., & Gould, W. S. Defense systems resources in the civil seeker. Washington, D.C.: U.S. Government Printing Office, 20402, cited by Boffey, P. M. systems analysis: No panacea for nation's domestic problems. *Science,* 1967, **158,** 1028-1030.

Goffman, E. *Asylums.* Garden City, N.J.: Doubleday, 1961.

Gomberg, W. The trouble with democratic management. *Trans-Action,* 1966, **3,** (5), 30-35.

Gross, G. M. The coming general systems models of social systems. *Human Relations,* 1967, **20,** 357-374.

Gurin, G., Veroff, J., & Feld, S. *Americans view their mental health.* New York: Basic Books, 1960.

Hall, R. H. Some organizational considerations in the professional-organizational relationship. *Administrative Science Quarterly,* 1967, **12,** 461-478.

Harrington, M. The social-industrial complex. *Harper's,* 1967, **235** (1410), 55-60.

Harshbarger, D. From chronic wards to therapeutic communities: II. The struggle for survival. *Hospital and Community Psychiatry,* 1967, **18,** 310-314.

Harshbarger, D. High priests in hospitaldom. *Hospital and Community Psychiatry,* 1970, **21,** 156-159. (a)

Harshbarger, D. The human service organization. Unpublished manuscript, Department of Psychology, West Virginia University, 1970. (b)

Harshbarger, D. An investigation of a structural model of small group problem solving. *Human Relations,* 1971, in press.

Hilleboe, H. E. Public health in the United States in the 1970's. *American Journal of Public Health,* 1968, **58,** 1588-1610.

Hirschowitz, R. G. Changing behavior in the state hospital organization. *Psychiatric Quarterly,* 1969, **43,** 591-611.

Hirschowitz, R. G. From chronic wards to therapeutic communities: I. Preparing and developing staff. *Hospital and Community Psychiatry,* 1967, **18,** 304-309.

Hochbaum, G. W. Consumer participation in health planning: Toward conceptual clarification. *Journal of the American Public Health Association,* 1969, **59,** 1698-1705.

Hofstadter, R. The future of American violence. *Harper's,* 1970, **240,** (1439), 47-53.

Howard, D. S. Relationships between governmental and voluntary agencies. *Encyclopedia of Social Work,* New York: National Association of Social Workers, 1965.

Kopkind, A. The future planners. *New Republic,* 1967, **156,** (8), 19-23.

Kornhauser, W. *Scientists in industry: Conflicts and accommodation.* Berkeley: University of California Press, 1962.

Kristol, I. Decentralization for what? *The Public Interest,* 1968, **II,** 17-25.

Lawrence, P. R., & Lorsch, J. W. Differentiation and integration in complex organizations. *Administrative Science Quarterly,* 1967, **12,** 1-47.

Levine, S., & White, P. E. Exchange as a conceptual framework for the study of interorganizational relationships. *Administrative Science Quarterly,* 1961, **5.**

Levine, S. Organizational and professional barriers to interagency planning. In Planning responsibilities of state departments of public welfare. Proceedings of a conference at Brandeis University, 1966.

Likert, R. *New patterns of management.* New York: McGraw-Hill, 1961.

Likert, R. *The human organization.* New York: McGraw-Hill, 1967.

Litwak, E., & Hylton, L. F. Interorganizational analysis: A hypothesis on coordinating agencies. *Administrative Science Quarterly,* 1962, **6,** 395-426.

Logue, E. J. The power of negative thinking. *Boston,* 1969, **61,** (2), 36-38, 57-61.

Mackenzie, R. A. The management process in 3-D. *Harvard Business Review,* 1969, **47** (6).

Mann, F. C. Studying and creating change: A means to understanding social organization. *Research in Industrial Human Relations,* Industrial Relations Research Association, 1957.

Mattison, B. Political implications in good public health administration. *American Journal of Public Health,* 1965, **55,** (2), 183-189.

Merton, R. K. Role of the intellectual in public bureaucracy. *Social theory and social structure,* Glencoe, Ill.: Free Press, 1957.

Michael, D. N. Social engineering and the future environment. *American Psychologist,* 1967, **22,** 888-892.

Mott, B. J. F. The myth of planning without politics. *American Journal of Public Health,* 1969, **59,** 797-803.

Moynihan, D. P. What is community action? *The Public Interest,* 1966, **5,** 3-8.

Murphy, C. G. Community organization for social welfare. *Social Work Yearbook,* 1960, **14,** 186-190.

Myrdal, G. *Asian drama: An inquiry into the poverty of nations.* New York: Twentieth Century Fund, 1968. 3 vols.

National Commission on Community Health Services. *Health administration and organizations in the decade ahead.* Washington, D.C.: Public Affairs Press, 1967.

National Information Bureau. *The volunteer board member in philanthropy.* New York: 1968.

Newman, E., & Demone, H. W., Jr. Policy paper—A new look at public planning for human services. *Journal of Health and Social Behavior,* 1969, **10,** 142-149.

Noble, J. H., Jr. Protecting the public's privacy in computerized health and welfare information systems. *Social Work,* 1971, **21** (1), 35-41.

O'Donnell, E., & Sullivan, M. Service delivery and social action through the neighborhood center: A review of research. *Welfare In Review,* 1969, **7,** 1-12.

Peattie, L. Reflections on advocacy planning. *American Institute of Planners Journal,* 1968, **34,** 80-88.

Perlman, R., & Jones, D. *Neighborhood Service Centers.* Washington, D.C.: Office of Juvenile Delinquency, Department of Health, Education and Welfare, 1967.

Peter, L., and Hull, R. *The Peter principle.* New York: Morrow, 1969.

Platt, J. What we must do. *Science,* 1969, **166,** 1115-1121.

Pray, K. L. M. When is community organization social work practice? In D.S. Howard (Ed), *Community organization: Its nature and settings.* New York: American Association of Social Workers, 1947.

Rand, G. What psychology asks of urban planning. *American Psychologist,* 1969, **24,** 929-935.

Rein, M., & Miller, S. M. Social action on the installment plan. *Trans-Action,* 1966, **3** (2), 31-32.

Rice, A. K. *The enterprise and its environment.* London: Tavistock Publications, 1958.

Roethlisberger, F. J. *Management and morale.* Cambridge: Harvard University Press, 1941.

Ross, M. G. *Community organization: Theory and principles.* New York: Harper, 1955.

Rothman, J. An analysis of goals and roles in community organization practice. *Social Work,* 1964, **9** (2), 24-31.

Sanders, I. T. Theories of community development. *Rural Sociology,* 1958, **23.**

Schaefer, M. Politics and public health. Unpublished doctoral dissertation in Public Administration, Syracuse University, 1962.

Scheff, T. J. Toward a sociological model of consensus. *American Sociological Review,* in press.

Schorr, D. *Don't get sick in America.* Nashville, Tenn.: Aurora Publishers, 1970.

Shick, A. The cybernetic state. *Trans-Action,* 1970, **7** (4), 15-26.

Sheldon, A., Baker, F., & McLaughlin, C. P. (Eds.) *Systems and medical care,* Cambridge, Mass.: MIT Press, 1970.

Simon, H., Smithburg, D. W., & Thompson, V. A. *Public administration.* New York: Knopf, 1961.

Slater, P., & Bennis, W. Democracy is inevitable. *Harvard Business Review,* 1964, **42** (2), 51-59.

Slater, P. *The pursuit of loneliness; American culture at the breaking point.* Boston: Beacon Press, 1970.

Sonthoff, H. What is the manager? *Harvard Business Review,* 1964, **42** (6), 24-36.

Spivack, M., & Demone, H. W., Jr. Mental health facilities: A model for physical planning. *Social Science and Medicine,* 1970, **3,** 513-528.

Stahl, O. G. *Public personnel administration.* New York: Harper, 1962.

Sussman, M. B. The sociologist as tool of social action. In A. Shostok (Ed.), *Sociology in Action.* Homewood, Ill. Dorsey Press, 1966.

Taubenhaus, L. J., Hamlin, R. H., & Wood, R. C. Performance reporting and program budgeting: Tools for program evaluation. *American Journal of Public Health,* 1957, **47,** 423-438.

Taylor, F. W. *The principles of scientific management.* New York: Harper, 1923.

Terreberry, S. The evolution of organizational environments. *Administrative Science Quarterly,* 1968, **12,** 590-613.

The American Assembly. The ombudsman. Meeting at Columbia University, October, 1967.

Thompson, J. D. *Organizations in action.* New York: McGraw-Hill, 1967.

Thompson, P. H., & Dalton, G. W. Performance appraisal: Managers beware. *Harvard Business Review,* 1970, **48** (1), 149-157.

Toffler, A. Coping with future shock. *Playboy,* 1970, **17** (3), 88-99 ff.

Torrens, P. R. A pilot program in coordination of care between an urban teaching hospital and the community's general practitioners. *American Journal of Public Health,* 1969, **59,** 60-64.

Townsend, R. *Up the organization.* New York: Knopf, 1970.

Von Bertalanffy, L. General systems theory. *General systems.* Yearbook of the society for the advancement of general systems theory, 1956, **1,** 1-10.

Walsh, J. Foundations: Taking stock after the Tax Reform Bill. *Science,* 1970, **167,** 1598-1599.

Warren, R. L. Types of social change at the community level. *Papers in Social Welfare,* 1965, No. 11. Walth im Mass., Brandeis University.

Warren, R. The interorganizational field as a focus for investigation. *Administrative Science Quarterly,* 1967, **12,** 396-419.

Warren, R. L. The mental health drama: Hamlet or Hellzapoppin? Paper presented at National Institute of Mental Health Regional Office Staff Meeting, Dallas, October 1969.

World Health Organization. Suggested outline for use by countries in discussing health education of the public. *A 12/Technical discussion/I,* March 31, 1958.

DATE DUE

5-25-77			
NOV 1 6 1977			
GAYLORD			PRINTED IN U.S.A.